THE IMAGINATION GAP

We are going to need to use our imagination to solve the biggest problems facing our world. We know imagination is one of the most powerful tools we have. Kids use it. Many adults have lost it. This book will help all of us to recapture, use and apply our imagination the best way we can.

— *Aria Finger, CEO, DoSomething.org*

Imagination is one of the greatest gifts we have - the ability to look at something one way and see it completely differently. And yet somehow in the transition to adulthood we often stop using our imagination. This book offers the encouragement and support we need to harness our collective imagination again and use it to change the world.

— *Rebecca Wainess, Director, Corporate Citizenship at Kenneth Cole Productions*

We have more access to information than in any time in human history. It's tempting to look at all that information to model solutions for the future. In *The Imagination Gap*, Brian Reich challenges that, while we can learn from the past, we must IMAGINE new solutions for the future, we must take risks and find comfort in the fear of the unknown. This book will reprogram your mind to imagine and dream big again.

— *Ash Greyson, Founder & Chief Evangelist at Ribbow Media*

Imagination is the next big thing, and Brian Reich has given imagination the attention it deserves. He explains why imagination is a critical to our success, in business, education, politics, media, and every other sector, and what it will take to harness our imagination as never before. Ignore this conversation at your own peril.

— *Malcolm Netburn, Chairman & CEO, CDS Global (a Hearst Company)*

As kids, we are encouraged to have a big imagination. As we get older, we're told not to let our imagination get the best of us. In his new book, *The Imagination Gap*, Brian Reich challenges that notion by reminding us that we need our imagination to make sense of the world, and deal with the challenges we encounter. The stakes are too high to not use our imagination. Reich shows us when and how to unleash our imagination, encourages us all to dream bigger, and challenges us to use the power of imagination to change the world.

— *Kari Saratovsky, Principal, Third Plateau Social Impact Strategies*

Every day, corporations, social entrepreneurs and nonprofits are doing innovative work to improve the lives of communities around the globe. In doing so, they are utilizing their imaginations and amplification powers to help create the kind of future we all want and deserve. We can all be part of this important work and we can do so by using and applying our own. Brian Reich has given imagination the attention it deserves and provides a well-thought out roadmap to help each of us harness our imagination as never before.

— *Susan McPherson - serial connector, cause marketer, angel investor,*
and corporate responsibility expert (also founder and CEO of McPherson Strategies)

Brian Reich shatters the construct that 'imagination' is merely a creative thinking exercise by reimagining imagination itself for what it truly is: The most powerful tool at our disposal to address the challenges facing our society. In a deeply intellectual and accessible way, Reich explains why imagination is critical to our success – in business, education, politics, and media — and what it will take to help us all unlock the power of our imagination and change the world.

— *Darren Grubb, Former Deputy Chief of Staff, U.S. Department of Commerce*

No one in the social change sector is better equipped than Brian Reich to offer advice about how think differently about problems we face today. He gives us a method to explore new, big, ambitious ideas, develop new models and the techniques for stretching our imagination.

— *Beth Kanter, The Happy Healthy Nonprofit: Strategies for Impact without Burnout*

The only way we will be able to truly advance the social causes and missions needed for our communities is to think differently about the challenges and solutions. Doing so can be incredibly intimidating. I hope Imagination Gap becomes a resource for community leaders of all kinds.

— *Amy Sample Ward, Executive Director of NTEN*

THE IMAGINATION GAP

BY
BRIAN REICH

United Kingdom – North America – Japan
India – Malaysia – China

Emerald Publishing Limited
Howard House, Wagon Lane, Bingley BD16 1WA, UK

Second edition 2018

Reprints and permissions service
Contact: permissions@emeraldinsight.com

British Library Cataloguing in Publication Data
A catalogue record for this book is available from the British Library

ISBN: 978-1-78714-207-7 (Hardback)
ISBN: 978-1-78769-098-1 (Paperback)
ISBN: 978-1-78714-206-0 (Online)
ISBN: 978-1-78714-306-7 (EPub)

ISOQAR certified
Management System,
awarded to Emerald
for adherence to
Environmental
standard
ISO 14001:2004.

Certificate Number 1985
ISO 14001

FSC
www.fsc.org
MIX
Paper from
responsible sources
FSC® C013604

INVESTOR IN PEOPLE

Contents

About the Author

Brian Reich is a strategist and writer for executive leaders at global brands, media companies, startups, nonprofits, and political organizations. His research and views regarding the impact of media and technology on society have been published in *The New York Times, Fast Company, Fortune, TechCrunch, Stanford Social Innovation Review, Vice, Wired, AdAge, The Chronicle of Philanthropy,* and others. He has delivered analysis of digital, media, political, and other trends on NPR and Fox News. Brian is also the author of *Shift & Reset: Strategies for Addressing Serious Issues in a Connected Society* and *Media Rules! Mastering Today's Technology to Connect with and Keep Your Audience.* Brian has held senior roles at leading PR, marketing, advertising, digital, and public affairs agencies and was briefing director for Vice President Al Gore in the White House. He serves as an advisor to several nonprofit organizations and startups. He attended the University of Michigan and holds a bachelor's degree in political science from Columbia University. He lives in New York City with his wife, Karen Dahl, and their two children.

Introduction

The most powerful forces in shaping and motivating people's behaviors and the shape of our society are all products of our imagination. However, even as the challenges and opportunities are greater than ever, we find ourselves using and applying our imagination less and less.

In my previous book, *Media Rules!*, I discussed the growing obsession with technology as a marketing and communications tool. The central argument was that three things — information, experiences, and stuff — have always driven people's decision-making, and that would always be true no matter what advances unfold in media or technology. Information is what fuels how we learn and make sense of our world; experiences are how we interact and form personal connections; and stuff is stuff. Products. The things we keep and wear and drive and more. Regardless of platform, regardless of channel or tool, one or all of these three things will play a critical role when you try to motivate someone to understand an idea or take an action.

When you are working to influence someone, to compel a certain action, the desired outcome falls under the umbrella of impact. The word "impact" is often applied to social good — but it applies much more broadly. Impact happens when you create something new. You have an impact when you change something. One time. Consistently. Sustainably. The impact can be big or small, and can take on all different forms. Some impacts will be obvious while others may be difficult to measure — and in most cases the significance of what happens in the world cannot be easily quantified. You can have an impact in a single moment, or see it play out over time.

One thing is clear about impact: it doesn't happen in isolation. We are all connected, so anything that happens has implications for everyone. Everything good that happens has the possibility of benefiting everyone, while everything bad affects us all in some ways as well.

In everything we do, personally or professionally, individually or collectively, we should consider the impact. In addition, we should strive to make a big impact in everything we do — to ensure that our ideas spread far and wide, our actions benefit as many people as possible. Unfortunately, that does not happen enough. There is plenty of talk about big goals and changing the world. However, we measure results quarter to quarter and project to projects, and rarely take the time to consider the larger impact. Words like transformation and disruption are used a lot, but the massive impact that seems possible is rarely achieved.

The problem is with our imagination. We aren't using or applying our imagination to the full extent possible. We talk about technology as having the potential to save the world and evolve everything about how we communicate and function as humans. Then we celebrate the efforts that prioritize short-term thinking and increased awareness — refusing to accept that the actual, meaningful, measurable impact on our lives is minimal at best. The problems that we face as a society will not be solved with short-term thinking. The idea of achieving world peace, ending the global refugee crisis, eradicating hunger or curing disease — these are massive challenges that have significant negative consequences, and society is not currently capable of stopping them. But, they aren't beyond the reach of our imagination. Amazing potential advancements in how to solve complex problems are not beyond the reach of our imagination.

Unfortunately, we aren't using or applying our imagination to its fullest. Instead, we are doing what we know. What we have always done — maybe with greater efficiency or scale. We are doing the things we have proven will work to varying degrees, that are easy to replicate. It is really easy to regurgitate things that we have become comfortable doing. Doing new things is much more difficult. That is where the potential for incredible impact exists — in doing new, ambitious, imaginative things.

The promise of imagination is achieving something that has never been done. Our imagination can help us explore new ways of thinking and operating that can move us well beyond what we are presently doing.

We Aren't Shooting for the Big Stuff

We live in a time of unprecedented possibility. Nevertheless, even though we have greater power to explore and experiment, and a chance to create an entirely different future, too much of our individual and collective focus is on what is happening right now. There are changes and improvements occurring every day, advances in health care that are extending life and media that is pushing people to think critically. However, we aren't creating entirely new ways of doing business. We aren't eradicating diseases. We have become comfortable with the idea that constant movement and incremental change is a sign of impact and progress and that that is enough. We have all but given up on the idea of solving the most complex problems.

We aren't using our imagination. There is a gap between what we think about, the kind of impact we try to have, and what we could conceivably achieve. We have an imagination gap. We are not going to get to have the kind of impact that is possible until we close that gap.

Everybody has an imagination. Everybody is born with an extraordinarily powerful tool to dream up things that nobody else can fully understand or appreciate. Our brain is far and away the most powerful tool that exists with unlimited capacity to generate new and transformative ideas only when it's activated and applied. Not only aren't we using our imagination as we could, we are actively shutting down others' imagination. We have revoked the privilege we have to be imaginative.

Think about what it was like when you were a kid. Take a few minutes to watch how a young child plays, learns, and explores the world around them. You will be in awe of the stories they create, the scenarios they dream up, the adventures their imagination takes them on. They are not trying to impress anyone or worrying about how they fit in. They don't just mimic what they see on television, quote someone who spoke to them, or follow instructions they were given — they also invent entirely original languages, people, and places. Most importantly, they are not being told that what they are doing is wrong. That comes later. Thanks to the power of their imagination, kids operate in a world of their own creation where anything is possible.

Now, think about your own experience. How often do you let your brain go in whatever direction it wants? How many times have you raised your hand in a meeting, or at a brainstorming session, and shared a truly novel idea? How many times have you thought of something wildly different, but kept quiet about it? Have you been told that your question is stupid or off topic, or your idea impossible to achieve? Our imagination is always working, always active — but we have become accustomed to suppressing our imagination, because what it produces doesn't align with others, or seems too big, too complicated, or not "on budget." Every time we are told that our ideas don't have merit, a little part of our imagination goes dark. Our willingness to use and apply imagination diminishes.

The good news is this: you can't kill imagination. The parts of your brain that generate new ideas will always be active. However, the more we suppress our imagination, or shut down others who try to share theirs, the larger the imagination gap becomes.

Permission to Use Your Imagination

You now have permission to use your imagination. You have permission to dream up new things. You have permission to propose ideas that do more than just improve a little on what we already know. You have permission to ask questions that don't have easily or available answers. In addition, you have permission to use and pursue things that have never been conceived of before, and probably don't seem like they're possible. When you do that, you are using your imagination. When you do that, you will put yourself, and all of us, on a very different track.

Some important things to keep in mind as you move ahead:

— *Imagination is not the same thing as creativity.* Creativity is a wonderfully powerful tool that we can activate to come up with messages and drawings and all sorts of stuff. That is a way to employ or express our imagination. That is not imagination.

— *Imagination is not the same as intelligence or experience.* You cannot be more or less imaginative than someone else (and you shouldn't believe someone who tells you as much). Every single one of us has exactly the same power to use our imagination and the same unlimited potential to put it to work.

— *Imagination = a new idea.* There are big ideas and small ideas, good ideas and bad ideas. The ways that we define and judge ideas is almost entirely subjective. What distinguishes imagination and differentiates it from everything else is the newness of the idea.

— *Imagination isn't a special talent or skill.* There is no certificate program you can complete to master using and applying your imagination. There aren't nine steps, or five principles or a certain color LEGO that, when used by everyone, will make them more imaginative. The more you fill your brain with — and the more diverse your experiences and inputs — the more you feed your imagination. If you try to engineer your thinking or force your brain to produce a specific solution, you will end up curbing your imagination more than anything.

— *Imagination is not the same as innovation.* Innovation is about solving problems and finding ways to change, improve, maximize, and optimize everything we do. Imagination is about creating things and ideas that are new — and may lead to innovation. Imagination is not about risk tolerance, or problem solving. Imagination is about going beyond what we know and can conceive is possible.

We can do more to use and apply our imagination, individually and collectively. Start by acknowledging that you have an imagination. Believe that it is amazing. Stop suppressing your imagination, or letting others impact your ability to explore and dream.

Imagination is a natural resource. It is not a thing, a process, or a system. It is not a plan, or a strategy, or a process that you can follow or implement. Imagination is a raw material that we can use for whatever we want. Every single germ of an idea starts with our imagination.

Starting Blocks

1) *Imagination happens. Let it.* I have to stop myself from suggesting ideas or "improvements" to my daughter that might influence the elaborate, interstellar war that is happening throughout our apartment with strategically placed stuffed animals and Magna-Tiles. She doesn't need my help. Nobody should try to force others to use imagination in the same way that they would. Just let it happen. Let it play out. There is so much to learn if you aren't interrupting yourself or others, while they are using their imagination.

2) *Don't listen to anyone else.* Your boss gets to say how many hours you work, decide how much you earn, dictate that you're working on a certain client, and direct you to be in Des Moines tomorrow for a meeting. He or she does not get to tell you that your imagination is good or not good, practical or not practical. Moreover, it is exactly that process — our teacher saying that's not how we measure success, our parents saying that's not appropriate behavior — it's those things

that slowly have stripped away our permission to use our imagination. In addition, if you think about the people who we revere for being the most imaginative, they're seeing the world in a way that nobody else sees it. They're using their imaginations to create solutions to complex challenges, and in many cases developing new ideas to make life better where the rest of us couldn't even conceive of the possibilities.

3) *Write it down.* Or draw it. Or pull out a recorder and start talking. Take the stupid, crazy ideas that are popping into your head and capture them. Each of those is an ingredient that needs to be kept somewhere besides your brain. Your memory is not there to spin off the good story, your memory is there to take facts and experiences and recall them. So if something new comes out, grab it. You may not know what to do with it now, but it's not going to come out in that exact same way again. So stop and write it down.

4) *Share it.* Don't share your imaginative idea(s) for validation purposes. Don't share them because you want to get hired or impress someone, or so you can show that your imagination is better than someone else's imagination. Share because the little piece of information that comes out of your head has power. That little piece of imagination goes into my head and changes the way my imagination is going to work. Ideas build on each other. That ingredient is going to mix with some other ingredients. If you keep it all to yourself, you may have an incredibly vibrant imagination but you're not going to inspire anyone else. The mornings when my son gets up, and we have a conversation, or play a game with imaginary characters or outcomes, my energy, focus, and my ability to generate new thoughts for the day are greater because I'm part of a shared imagination experience.

Imagination is infectious, and deserves to be shared. You don't need a group to have an imagination. You can't pull a task force together; fill a room with different people who can collectively generate an imaginative idea. But you can share your imagination. Moreover, you should.

5) *Embrace your imagination as it is.* Don't worry about the practicality of what pops into your head. Don't worry about all the crazy steps that you're going to have to take the idea that your imagination has generated from start to finish. Imagination is not triggered when you force it. Your imagination fires when you're in the shower, because it's the only quiet time that your brain gets during the day. Your imagination flourishes when you spend time in the great outdoors, away from the noise and chaos of everyday life, because you've broken your normal daily routine. It's not because you're in the forest, or you're closer to God, or the weather is nice — it's because you have broken your pattern. And that's the moment at which your imagination has an opportunity to come out again.

Don't go camping to go camping, but if you go camping, listen a little bit closer to your brain, and bring a piece of paper so that you don't forget what you thought of when you saw that animal, or tree, or whatever you do when you camp. I don't camp.

How to Read This Book

The book you are about to read begins with an introduction to imagination and the important role it plays in all aspects of our lives — personally, professionally, and more broadly as a community. Each successive chapter takes on the specific challenges that need to be addressed, from acknowledging and understanding that an imagination gap exists to the steps that need to be considered in order to close the gap.

If we can use and apply our imagination more, our ability to think and act differently and develop new and better ideas will improve. Every one of us has an imagination, and we all can do more to use and apply our imagination. Closing the imagination gap will benefit everyone — government and political organizations, news and media, entertainment, sports, marketers and advertisers, educational institutions, thought leaders, brands and corporations, nonprofits, foundations, and charities, as well as each of us individuals.

In researching and writing this book, I conducted interviews with more than two-dozen scientists, entrepreneurs, organizational leaders, subject matter experts and practitioners, as well as actors, filmmakers, comedians, inventors, and others whose experiences and insights provide powerful evidence to support the need to close the imagination gap. I have also weaved together media coverage, research, and personal experiences. Moreover, to whatever extent possible, my analysis includes recent events whose outcomes were uncertain as we went to print.

The goal of *The Imagination Gap* is to spark real changes in our behavior. I want you to expand the use of your imagination, and help the people you know, work with, and serve to do the same. More broadly, I believe we can change how individuals and organizations think, operate and communicate, by helping them to close *The Imagination Gap* and unlock the potential that exists (but is not currently being fully realized). To help balance the big thinking with practical insights and actions that anyone can take, each chapter also includes:

— A summary of the critical ideas included in each chapter to help organize and prompt you to think about different ways to use and apply your imagination.

— An "imagination challenge" that encourages you to use and apply your imagination. The challenges include questions, prompts, and directives that will help to take the discussion beyond the pages of the book and into your life and work.

I will also continue to share relevant, timely, compelling, interesting, fun, or other information about using and applying your imagination at www.theimaginationgap.com

I wrote this book to be a resource that you can have on your desk, on your phone, keep next to your bed, or carry around with you in your bag. I hope the book is not only informative and interesting, but also useful and applicable. You can read the book from cover to cover, dog-ear, and highlight different pages and passages. You can also pick out different sections that you find valuable now, and come back later to read (or reread) passages in the future when they seem more applicable. Each person who reads this book will bring his or her own experiences and perspectives to this discussion.

This Book Is Like My Brain

I spend a lot of my time exploring how people get and share information and the role that technology plays in how we spend our time. My work focuses on how to get people to think a certain way, vote, donate, buy something, tell someone, volunteer, read, watch, or listen to anything. My passion is behavior change — getting people to think and act differently than they currently do. I also have a sense of personal responsibility to doing something with a positive and meaningful impact on the world that motivates much of this work and my beliefs.

The stories, interviews, examples, facts, quotes, numbers, personal observations, and more that you find in the pages that follow reflect my curiosity, my work, my relationships, and my perspective on the world. I have written a book that reflects how my brain works, and what my imagination dreams up.

I want you to feel excited about the prospect of having and sharing ideas that other people might not fully understand or appreciate. I want you to feel confident that the ideas that you have, whatever your imagination offers up, has value. With the help of this book, you will be able to take the steps so that the rest of us benefit from your imagination as well.

I also want you to squirm a bit when reading this book because you consider how your individual behaviors could change; you might alter your approach. That's when things will start to look different. That's when the real fun begins. That's when your imagination will be most engaged.

When this happens, when we make imagination something that is expressed, shared, and valued by everyone the way it can and should be, amazing things are going to happen.

You don't have to believe me. Read the book to see for yourself.

Acknowledgments

I have a lot of people to thank and recognize for their support and contribution to the writing of this book.

First and foremost, I want to thank you for reading the book. I want to thank you in advance for using your imagination, sharing your ideas, and helping to carry this conversation forward.

I am deeply grateful to the entire team at Emerald Group Publishing for their support to this project, for their patience, and for their efforts to smooth and polish the language in the book and make it worthy of publication.

I sincerely appreciate all the people who interviewed for the book for their willingness to share their intelligence and insights with me. These people challenged my thinking, informed my views, and provided me with evidence of what was possible when you use and apply your imagination. The long and illustrious list of people who contributed to the book include:

Macky Alston, Documentary filmmaker

Noah Brier, CEO and co-founder of Percolate

Jeff Degraff, Dean of innovation, University of Michigan

Bradley Feinstein, Co-founder and president at Dropel Fabrics

Harrison Greenbaum, Stand-up comedian

Michael Gump, Prop master, art director, Instagram sensation

Bryan Johnson, Entrepreneur

Rita King, Founder – Director, Science House

Isaac Luria, Movement leader, faith-rooted organizer, social impact technologist

Josh Linkner, Entrepreneur, author, speaker

Peter McGraw, Behavioral scientist and author of *The Humor Code*

Marty Neumeier, Director of transformation, *Liquid Agency*

John Porch, Stand-up comedian

Doug Rauch, Founder of Daily Table, former president of Trader Joe's

Kurt Ronn, Creative entrepreneur, philanthropist

Jamie Rose, Photographer

Alec Ross, Author and former innovation advisor, U.S. State Department

Jason Rosenkrantz, Multimedia storyteller

Nathan Sawaya, Artist, LEGO brick artist

Hannah Scott, Lab co-cordinator, Hungry Mind Lab

Johanna Schwartz, Documentary filmmaker

Peter Shankman, Public relations all-star, entrepreneur, author

Jake Siewert, Global head of corporate communications, Goldman Sachs

Dia Simms, President, President — Combs Wine & Spirits

Sree Sreenivasan, Former chief digital officer, Metropolitan Museum of Art

Sarah Stiles, Tony-nominated actress

Darya Zabelina, PhD — University of Colorado Boulder, Institute of Cognitive Science

There are plenty of other people who did not interview for the book, but still provided recommendations, shared stories, recommended books and articles, and generally contributed to my research and writing. Thank you to everyone who joined me on this journey and put your imagination to work as well.

I am fortunate to have a group of friends and advisors willing to provide advice, as well as just the right dose of reality when I need it most. They include Michael Slaby, Merrill Brown, Ari Wallach, Kathleen Hessert, Dan Solomon, Maged Bishara, Liba Rubenstein, Kari Saratovsky, Darren Grubb, Donny Furst, Scott Henderson, Malcolm Netburn, Matt Cerrone, Paul Orzulak, and Doug Weinbrenner.

I also want to thank the people who have hired me, worked with me, encouraged me, challenged me, and provided me with a laboratory for testing and refining my ideas over the past two years. They include Sean "Diddy" Combs, Natalie Moar (and the team at Combs Enterprises), Keith Clinkscales (and the team at REVOLT), Anne-Marie Grey (and the team at the United States for UNHCR), Ryan Seacrest and Kelly Brown, Malcolm Netburn, Robbie Salter, Mark Katz, everyone at Bethesda Softworks, Phillip Morelock (and the team at Playboy), Kathleen Hessert, Stu Loeser, Jonathan Fassberg, Cherie Greer Brown, and more.

I want to thank my mother, Ann Sheffer, for regularly asking me what the book was about (either because she forgot or because she was curious, I'm not sure it matters) — which forced me to refine and improve my thesis. I also want to thank my father, Jay Reich, for discussing and debating the issues addressed in the book with me, and pushing me (without even realizing he was doing it) to raise the level of my argument.

Finally, I want to thank the three most important people in my life.

My kids — Henry and Lucy — are the reason I wrote this book. They have incredible, boundless imaginations and helped me to understand the power of using and applying your imagination in ways that no study, interview, client or experiment could ever offer. They inspire me with their ideas and their ambition. They also provided helpful edits and suggestions on the language of the book itself. I hope that they never lose their curiosity and sense of wonder, and I hope that the rest of us do our part to close the imagination gap so that they will be able to use and apply their imaginations to shape the kind of future we all will benefit from. I love you both.

If not for my wife, Karen Dahl, this book would not have happened. That is not an exaggeration. She provided unwavering support from beginning to end, and limitless understanding and patience as I spent hours and hours researching, interviewing, writing, and editing the book. Karen has an endless reserve of patience, understanding, and love that is always available to me. Moreover, she is a talented writer and editor whose recommendations for, and revisions to, my writing made this book far, far better. I love you.

Thank you to everyone.

What Is Imagination?

This chapter explores the history and science behind imagination and the origins of imagination in ancient philosophy, and highlights how imagination works. When applied purposefully, imagination becomes a powerful force in driving people's creative abilities, decision-making capacity, and willingness to take action.

There is no single or perfect definition of imagination. We know that imagination is the ability to form new images and sensations in the mind. We know that those images and sensations are not the same as what our brain collects and processes through our senses such as when we hear or see something. We each have our own imagination, shaped by what we know and experience, and it exists entirely inside our brain.

Unless we share what our imagination creates, it remains an internal mechanism for each of us to view and process what is happening in the world. The word "imagination" comes from the Latin verb *imaginari* meaning "to picture oneself." Nobody can see your imagination or know that you are using it, unless you choose to unleash it on the world.

Imagination helps us conceive the world, our lives, and interact with people, and life, not as they are but as they could be. Imagination provides a window into the world of what is possible. Imagination can push us to think beyond what we know, where we are comfortable — to the unknown, and toward a future of our own creation.

Without imagination, our progress will always be limited. This is true for everyone: business/brands, political and advocacy groups, governments, media, nonprofit and charitable organizations, schools, families, individuals, — all of us. The imagination allows us to project ourselves beyond our own immediate space and time, by anticipating what dangers exist or trouble we might encounter. Imagination also allows us to envision the future, as individuals and as collectives.

Imagination is about invention and fostering new thinking and novel ideas. By contrast, creativity and innovation are applied in more practical and measurable ways. That distinction is important for many reasons: First, they are different — imagination comes before creativity and innovation, and it feeds those processes. Second, we need to be comfortable generating and pursuing ideas without knowing whether or not those ideas are valuable before they are fully considered. Our imagination helps us to function in the face of uncertainty.

As Hannah Scott, the co-coordinator of the Hungry Minds Lab explained, "Creativity is the production of something new and useful using imagination, so it cannot exist without it. Imagination, however, can exist without creativity because it's the first step in the process."[1] She also noted that we can't equate creative output (a directly observable variable) to imagination, because not all imaginative thinking makes it as far as creative output, and that while we haven't yet developed a full understanding of imagination, we do know that it influences human behavior and is different from person to person. "Any individual difference is worth measuring, in order to help us better understand ourselves."

A Brief History of Imagination

The earliest beliefs about imagination were through the lens of philosophy. It was seen as an intermediary between the real and perceived, what could be touched or otherwise experienced, and what we thought might be possible.

Aristotle, a Greek philosopher, believed the imagination served as a bridge between the images that we take in from the world and the ideas what we generate from inside ourselves. To Aristotle the imagination was constantly involved in our intellectual activity — something that we needed to form any thought or contemplate any idea.

In the 1200s, St. Thomas Aquinas, an Italian philosopher and theologian, also argued that the imagination acted as a mediator between mind and body, but warned that the imagination was a particularly weak part of the mind, and thus susceptible to influence or confusion. He wrote that "Demons are known to work on men's imagination, until everything is other than it is."[2]

Rene Descartes, the French mathematician and scientist who was considered the father of modern western philosophy, was dismissive of the value of imagination. In the 1600s, he wrote, "This power of imagination which I possess is in no way necessary to my essence ... for although I did not possess it I should still remain the same that I now am." He also wrote of "the misleading judgment that proceeds from the blundering constructions of the imagination."

In 1580, Phillip Sidney argued against criticism and fear among Puritans regarding fantasy saying that imagination had value. He explained, "Poetry is more philosophical than history, as the historian is trapped with facts. The poet uses the facts of the historian, but he makes them more noble by using the imagination in the creative process."[3] Sidney wasn't alone in this conception of imagination either — around the same time, William Blake, the English poet, said, "What is now proved was once only imagined."

Furthermore in the late 1700s, Immanuel Kant, the German philosopher, explained how imagination allows humans to supplement knowledge and shortcut the need for proof. For example, our imagination allows us to reason that even though we can't see all sides of a cube, we can still know that cube has six sides without picking it up to confirm. In other words, our imagination connects what is real and what is not yet real. He acknowledged that, "the imagination is a powerful agent for creating as it were a second nature out of the material supplied to it by actual nature."

It wasn't until the early 20th century that the discussion around imagination started to take on a more practical tone. Jean-Paul Sartre theorized that imagination must satisfy two requirements: "It must account for the spontaneous discrimination made by the mind between its images and its perceptions; and it must explain the role that images play in the operation of thinking." He argued that imagination differs from perception in that perception receives its objects, whereas imagination intentionally generates them. Imagination, he wrote, "is not an empirical and superadded power of consciousness, it is the whole of consciousness as it realizes its freedom."[4] It is Sartre's explanation of imagination that provides the foundation for our current thinking about imagination.

Imagination is about discovery, invention, and originality. Each of us has a unique imagination, and it can be used to inspire and influence others. Imagination provides us with the opportunity to think about what might be possible rather than just be limited to what we know is real. Our imagination informs our reality, by generating images and ideas of what the world is like, to supplement what we see, hear, and experience directly. And while imagination serves its own function, it also contributes to many other aspects of our lives and how we function as human beings.

Even science, which largely belongs to the domain of logical and analytical thinking, has progressed forward because of human imagination. If you look at the greatest scientific theories and discoveries, you will see that they were spurred by the use of the imagination and intuition. Rationality, logic, and mathematics are later used to verify (or disprove), structure and define conjectures and ideas.

Imagination Is Uniquely Human

Humans love to consider different scenarios. We can tell stories, picture future situations, empathize with others' experiences, contemplate potential explanations for why something has occurred, plan how to share knowledge or teach skills, and reflect on moral dilemmas. We can do all these things because of our imagination.

Imagination can be playful and fun with no consequence whatsoever other than generating ideas in your head. It can be subversive, convincing you that something is dangerous when it's not. It can make you see things differently and beyond the limitations of your reality. It can help you step beyond your perspective and look at a situation from different angles. It can invoke powerful visions that motivate you to move forward when you are stuck and unable to act.

Take a moment to watch a young child play alone and you will experience firsthand the magic that comes from imagination. Creative thought turns the mundane into a magical experience. It is what turns a simple box into a space shuttle, a laundry basket into a race car, and an evening bath into a deep sea exploration. Stuffed animals become patients as well as superheroes. An empty paper towel roll can be transformed into an outfit, a spy glass or an instrument. Kids do this for enjoyment, but also because it helps them make sense of the world. They learn and experience new things each day, and consider what might happen in the future, all by using their imagination. It is what makes them human.

There is some evidence that this basic capacity to simulate exists in other species. When rats are in a well-known maze, they seem to be able to think ahead and consider their options before making a decision how to proceed. Apes are able to learn and interpret human symbols, learning in much the same way that we seem to as humans. But Jacob Bronowski believes that imagination is what makes humans unique from animals. Bronowski was a Polish-born intellectual who was trained as a mathematician but eventually studied and wrote on the sciences, technology, poetry and the relationship between creativity in the arts and the sciences. In his essay, "The Reach of Imagination," he explained, "The tool that puts the human mind ahead of the animal is imagery." He wrote that humans possess a unique ability to create and remember images — the most important of which are words. "Animals do not have words, in our sense: there is no specific center for language in the brain of any animal, as there is in the human being."[5]

Bronowski concluded that the human imagination depends on a configuration in the brain that has only evolved in the last couple of million years. And while imagination makes it possible for humans to create a future that does not yet exist, and may never come to exist in that form, "By contrast, the lack of symbolic ideas, or their rudimentary poverty, cuts off an animal from the past and the future alike, and imprisons him in the present. Of all the distinctions between man and animal, the characteristic gift which makes us human is the power to work with symbolic images: the gift of imagination."[5]

Just as there is no single, perfect explanation of imagination, there isn't definitive evidence as to how imagination works or doesn't. There is also no way to confirm, one way or another, that animals don't possess imaginations. Arguably, suggesting that some species possess imagination while others do not could be considered evidence of a lack of imagination. And the same line of thinking must be considered when we think about the connection between imagination and faith, or our ability to empathize with other people, or collaborate — topics that will be addressed later in the book.

We also know that imagination contributes to the recall of an experience from our past, and can help us piece together several existing ideas into something new. But, imagination is not about what has already happened. What makes imagination unique, and so compelling, is when we use our imagination we are looking into the future and conceiving of things that aren't real (or aren't real yet).

People use the word imagination in different ways, often without giving real consideration to its meaning. The phrase "I can't imagine ..." or the question "Can you imagine ...?" is tossed about casually in conversation. People use imagination to describe when they are picturing something in their head, anticipating what could happen at an event they might attend later or how they might feel if X, Y, or Z happened to them. The word imagination is also confused with creativity and innovation.

But our imagination is not only engaged when we are creating art, anticipating danger, or trying to remember something that has occurred (or our version of how something occurred). We all have a unique imagination, and the ability to apply it in a range of different ways. Imagination is a key component of planning, comprehending language, designing, and believing. When a person uses their imagination, the many different parts of our brain are working together, making connections and fueling insights that influence our perception of the world — and potentially changing our behavior.

Eyes Forward

Everyone knows change is difficult, and occasionally painful. We have to force ourselves to try new things, whether implementing a new idea, testing a new piece of technology or engaging with people who aren't a part of our community. Most of us don't do enough or go far enough. So much of our change is incremental. So many of our experiments — attempts to change that we consider bold and exciting — are really just slight variations on common behaviors.

But imagination allows us to conceive of possibilities for the future. Our imagination changes how we make sense of the past and present. Without a new, bold, exciting vision for the future, nothing about our current approaches will change. Without change, there can't be progress.

Major advancements won't happen without real commitment, sacrifice, and hard work — but the most important ingredient is the ambition that comes with ideas that emerge from our imagination. We wouldn't have made it to the moon or invented the Internet if we were satisfied with small improvements on what already existed. Incremental change is important, especially because it can add up to something bigger, but a large shift needs to take place for real progress to happen. The big things don't just happen. We discover and achieve the most compelling, most exciting, new things because we use our imagination to set a new course.

Most people don't spend much time thinking about new things because they aren't rewarded for it. We don't appreciate the contribution that imaginative ideas have on everything else happening in our society. Without imagination, innovation isn't possible. Without imagination, there is no creativity. Without imagination, there won't be any new, groundbreaking developments in science, or medicine, art or music, education or even the simple things about how we live our lives.

You Can't Engineer Imagination

We all are faced with some form of imagination gap. There is some distance between what we are capable of dreaming up and where we spend most of our time focusing our thinking and directing our energy. This is the Imagination Gap. We don't spend enough time or energy considering what is possible beyond what is practical. We focus on solving the problems that exist today, making improvements on what we already know. We undermine our own approaches to creativity, innovation, and the other important contributors to progress by making our goals achievable and our ambitions reasonable.

There are an abundance of books, articles, and gurus explaining the value of innovation and creativity. There are structures, methodologies, and tools that so-called experts offer to help you achieve your desired outcomes. They all take a familiar shape: 5 Steps to a More Innovative Organization; 4 Stages of Creativity; 7 Rules for Being More Creative. The Internet provides a constant flow of ready access to information on any topic we might want to explore. But they all feed the same set of behaviors — trained on improving the lives that we already know and experience. While we may benefit from further optimizing things about how we live and work, that approach will not close the imagination gap.

We also will not close the imagination gap by going offline, rejecting technology, or setting aside designated times to think expansively. There is no schedule for when your imagination is most likely to be engaged and no methodology for forcing it to happen. The key is to break the pattern. Try new things. Force your brain to shift from one focus to the next so you scramble the signals. And when new and different connections are made, new and different ideas are born.

Imagination as We Experience It

Viktor Frankl, a Jewish psychiatrist, spent three horrific years during World War II living in several of the most notorious Nazi concentration camps. While imprisoned, Frankl realized he had one single freedom left: He had the power to determine his response to the horror unfolding around him. He chose to imagine his wife and the prospect of seeing her again. He chose to imagine himself teaching students after the war about the lessons he had learned. Frankl survived and went on to chronicle his experiences and the wisdom he had drawn from them in his 1946 book, *Man's Search for Meaning*. In the book he wrote "A human being is a deciding being. Between stimulus and response there is a space. In that space is our power to choose our response. In our response lies our growth and our freedom." The space that Frankl described is in the imagination. We all have that space, whether we actively use it or not, and no matter what we use it for. That space allows us to supplement our actual experiences and to create an alternate reality.

But imagination is not just for the creation of abstract ideas and new thoughts. What we imagine can alter how we perceive the world around us. Specifically, what we imagine hearing can change what we see, and what we imagine seeing can change what we hear. According to a study from the Karolinska Institutet in Sweden, "our imagination of a sound or a shape changes how we perceive the world around us in the same way actually hearing that sound or seeing that shape does".[6,7] In other words, if we decide something is real, even with no evidence to back that up, our imagination can convince us that it is real — to us.

Scientists and artists alike have demonstrated how allowing their imaginations the freedom to grow and evolve their thoughts results in outcomes that are very different than what they might already know. Their use of imagination has generated discoveries and creations that have changed the way we all live. Without imagination there wouldn't be books or television, cars, airplanes, space travel, the Internet — and countless other amazing inventions.

While we might not all be scientists and artists, imagination can play a very real and important role in everyday life. As adults we have been forced into a world of responsibility and practicality where paying the bills, and having a job (sometimes which we hate), dictate a lot about how we live and what we are able to experience about the world. By tapping into our imagination, we are able to envision other options, and explore what might be possible.

Similarly, imagination can be used to consider different scenarios that might arise in the future so that you can be prepared. Johanna Schwartz, an award-winning filmmaker who was named one of *Foreign Policy* magazine's "Global Thinkers" for 2016, applies this kind of future scenario planning when preparing a documentary. She explains:

> I'm running scenarios constantly in my brain. This could happen, this could happen, that could happen. This guy could say this and if he says this and my next question will be that. I'm constantly creating all of these worlds in my head of what might happen so that I'm mentally prepared. That is how I use my imagination.

Imagination can be used to create anything — a language, a special place, friends, and more. It can be applied in business, education, as part of the arts, or anything else. We can be in the same place and share an experience. We can use the same words or images and share a language. We can cocreate a product or collaborate to solve a problem and the output is a mashup of talents and effort. Our imagination also allows us to connect and appreciate what someone else might be experiencing. But you can't share an imagination. We all have our own experiences and our own imaginations. Our imagination helps us create a version of someone else's reality that we can compare to our own.

Innovation and Imagination Are Different

We're living in a time of unprecedented change. Every week, there are new apps to download, ideas to ponder, products to buy, or trends to embrace. We are also seeing major shifts in global politics, advancements in health, and changes in population — where people live, how they interact, and what that does to our ecosystem. Much of the credit for the change that we are experiencing has been given to technology. Companies like Microsoft, Apple, Google, Amazon, Facebook, and more recently Tesla, Uber, Airbnb, and others are held up as the most dynamic leaders in the push toward the future. Some of that credit for transforming the planet is deserved — the desktop computer, the mobile phone, e-commerce, and eventually things like the driverless car will have a substantial impact on the shape of our existence.

But just how transformative were these creations? All of these exciting improvements to our lives qualify as innovations — necessary and valuable improvements on the way that we had operated in the past. Information is more available and certain luxuries more accessible than ever before. Even the most successful of these ventures are still reaching a relatively small number of people. A little over a billion people use Facebook on a regular basis — but that means more than five times as many do not. Google reports that more than 187 million unique users conduct over 3.5 billion searches each day — but on a planet with more than 7 billion residents, the vast majority are still seeking out information from other sources.

Buoyed by the successes of these companies, their products, and the methodology that they follow, innovation has become one of the most widely embraced concepts of recent history — and not just in the technology sector, or business world — by virtually everyone.

Books about innovation are published weekly. Every organization, regardless of size or industry, has seemingly embraced the idea (or in some cases the need) to innovate. Some of the most powerful innovators in history, ranging from GE to Honda to Google, have connected involvement in innovation initiatives to career development, incentives, and promotion because innovation is what they expect from their future leaders. There is no part of the global society that is immune to the pressure to innovate.

The thinking goes: if we can only help people to be more creative, then the innovation will flow. With innovation as our driving force, the changes that we can drive will forever change the world. Furthermore, if we can only set the right conditions, anyone can produce ideas and solutions that have the potential to push our world forward. The products of the digital age, and the sharing economy, are certainly compelling. These and countless other innovations offer measurable improvements over the past. They are laudable for all that they have achieved, but ultimately limited in their reach and impact.

Like any other business function or discipline, we can learn a lot from pursuing innovation. We review our efforts, spot where we made critical breakthroughs and where we missed key insights. Finding ways to improve our lives is one of the most important things we can spend our time and resources pursuing. Innovation is a process, a structured approach to doing things differently — accelerating and enabling important changes to occur, and its applicable in all aspects of our lives and society.

I think innovation is great, but I also know it's not enough. There are too many problems that need to be solved and opportunities to get healthier, to develop billion dollar products, to change the way people think or behave that are not going to be achieved through innovation alone. Innovation thrives on small changes. It produces iterations of what we know and what we have determined no longer works, or could work better. These small and subtle innovations make a world of difference.

By contrast, imagination requires our brains to make connections between seemingly unrelated concepts, to produce new and novel ideas. Imagination is about doing things that have never been done before.

Why Is Imagination So Important Now?

The pace of change is so rapid that it is easy to become focused on this approach to innovation, the commitment to small, regular improvements that seemingly result in dramatic changes to our lives. When we focus on those issues, we often lose sight of the big picture. In times of massive change and constant disruption, it is more important than ever that we look further ahead, and consider the larger opportunities that could be available.

We have experienced these periods of major disruption before — and just as now, it was the use of imagination during those times that helped us to shape a future that was so dramatically different than what came before. A few examples:

In the mid-15th century in Mainz, Germany, Johann Gutenberg brought together a number of existing technologies to become the first printer to use moveable metal type in the Western world. The idea of capturing knowledge wasn't original — but the idea of printing books to share with the masses was beyond comprehension at the time. The idea was dismissed as unnecessary. But with the benefit of history, we know that the printing press accelerated the transition from the Middle Ages to the modern world. By facilitating the dissemination of human knowledge through mechanization, the printing press paved the way for the Renaissance, the Reformation, and the Scientific Revolution as well.

Fast forward to the Industrial Revolution and the idea that we could take the labor that was powering so much of the country and scale it. Until the late 1700s, manufacturing was often done in people's homes, using hand tools or simple machines. Then, around 1764, Englishman James Hargreaves invented the spinning jenny ("jenny" was another word for "engine"), a machine that enabled individuals to produce multiple spools of threads simultaneously. That invention began the march toward industrialization, which led to the establishment of modern transportation, communication, and banking systems.

And then came the information age — which is best known for the introduction of the Internet and mobile technology. In 1948, Norbert Wiener, an American mathematician at the Massachusetts Institute of Technology (MIT), published an essay titled "Cybernetics." Two years later, he wrote *The Human Use of Human Beings.* Together, those essays explored the potential of automation and the risks of dehumanization by machines. While machines had already replaced many human roles and functions across industries, the essays are considered landmark theoretical works that both foreshadowed and influenced the arrival of computing, robotics, and automation — the meshing of man and machine. As *The New York Times* noted "Wiener was not the only forward thinking scientist or mathematician considering the role that computers and robots would play in future society – but the publishing of his essay was a critical part of the evolution of the discussion. It was an important advancement, an incremental innovation in the discussion, that would mark the beginning of the Machine Age".[8,9]

Welcome to the Imagination Age

As the Industrial Revolution shaped and re-shaped our world in various ways for nearly two centuries, the information age has opened the door to the next great shift in our existence in a quarter of that time. We are now rapidly approaching what could be called The Imagination Age.

Designer and writer Charlie Magee first introduced the terms "imagination age" and "age of imagination" in 1993. In an essay entitled "The Age of Imagination: Coming Soon to a Civilization Near You" he argued that "the most successful groups throughout human history have had one thing in common: when compared to their competition they had the best system of communication".[10] He theorized that the most successful communities throughout history have been those with (a) the highest concentration of people with access to high quality information, (b) greater ability to transform that information into knowledge and action, and (c) freedom to communicate that new knowledge to the other members of their group. Our individual and collective ability to survive and thrive as the world hurdles forward will depend on our ability to extend full access to the tools and privileges to everyone. As Rita J. King, the co-director of Science House, wrote "Cultural transformation is a constant process, and the challenges of modernization can threaten identity, which leads to unrest and eventually, if left unchecked, to violent conflict. Under such conditions it is tempting to impose homogeneity, which undermines the highly specific systems that encompass the myriad luminosity of the human experience."

King has long advocated for the idea of an "Imagination Age," and tracked its emergence over time. In a 2008 essay entitled "Our Vision for Sustainable Culture in the Imagination Age,"[11] she wrote that "Active participants in the Imagination Age are becoming cultural ambassadors by introducing virtual strangers to unfamiliar customs, costumes, traditions, rituals and beliefs, which humanizes foreign cultures, contributes to a sense of belonging to one's own culture and fosters an interdependent perspective on sharing the riches of all systems."

When I interviewed King in June of 2016, she explained how her thinking on the subject has evolved over the years:

> I started working with leadership teams around the world and I realized that they all have the same problem regardless of industry: they were really entrenched in industrial era thinking. We were all raised and educated in an industrial era model. In the industrial era, things are tangible and heavy and they make sense. An engine works or it doesn't work. It's a very binary, a loom, a car.
>
> These are all things that work or don't work. A factory. The work day starts and ends in the industrial era. Now we are headed into an era where things are very nebulous and hard to understand. Algorithms, data, these are nebulous concepts. The work day does not start and end. It just bleeds over into life.
>
> We are going from a tangible, heavy, common sense reality in which people moved faster and faster and faster and your output, your profit, was greater if you got people to move faster. It's not like that anymore. But we don't know exactly what comes next. The Imagination Age acts as a bridge between the certainty of the industrial age and the future that hasn't been fully defined yet.

We are still trying to figure out how to get the most out of the technology (and all that is associated with it) that we have available — the Internet, big data, Virtual Reality, the systems, and software that power the sharing economy. We arguably haven't even started to apply those tools in the most interesting and most significantly valuable ways. As Jill Lepore wrote in the New Yorker, "Things you own or use that are now considered to be the product of disruptive innovation include your smartphone and many of its apps, which have disrupted businesses from travel agencies and record stores to mapmaking and taxi dispatch. Much more disruption, we are told, lies ahead."[12]

However, Lepore notes the ideas that have fueled so much innovation and disruption in business, and particularly the technology industry, are more difficult to apply in other sectors. "The logic of disruptive innovation is the logic of the startup: establish a team of innovators, set a whiteboard under a blue sky, and never ask them to make a profit, because there needs to be a wall of separation between the people whose job is to come up with the best, smartest, and most creative and important ideas and the people whose job is to make money by selling stuff," she writes. It will not succeed without that clear separation — that wall.

The wall — or as Rita J. King referred to it, that bridge — requires the use of our imagination. What is preventing us from more fully embracing technology and its disruptive potential, not just in business but across all aspects of our lives, is the Imagination Gap. Instead of exploring the boundless possibilities of using technology to advance health or re-invent global politics, the limits of our imagination result in apps that enable a better television viewing experience or on-demand food delivery. So many potentially interesting and important ideas are going unexplored or not even being introduced at all.

A Lack of Imagination Is Learned

In the 1960s, a creative performance researcher named George Land conducted a study of 1600 five-year-olds and 98% of the children scored in the "highly creative" range. Dr. Land re-tested each subject during five-year increments. When the same children were 10-years-old, only 30% scored in the highly creative range. This number dropped to 12% by age 15 and just 2% by age 25. As the children grew into adults they effectively had the creativity trained out of them. In the words of Dr. Land, "non-creative behavior is learned."[13]

The same is true when it comes to imagination. Macky Alston, the Vice President for Strategy, Engagement, and Media at Auburn Theological Seminary, explained to me how our experiences as we grow up impact our use of imagination:

> Grownups are so judged and self-critical, so terrified of losing our jobs and of being ostracized in our social circles, that we do almost anything, post-adolescence, to not rock the boat. We want to conform. We want to be popular. We want to get a raise. We want to get ahead. We watch what works and we replicate it. We try to make changes, big or small. But any kind of innovation often is a product of privilege and the innovators often are the ones who feel like they don't have the same amount to lose that others do, and so they're willing to take those risks. Or they have nothing to lose in another regard where they have been so pushed up against the wall by life that they say, "Fuck it. I will choose life over death because I've tasted death and I don't like it."

We are afraid. We are afraid to be wrong. We are afraid to make people angry. We are afraid to try something different. We are afraid to change. We are afraid of change. And we are afraid to use and apply our imagination — to put our ideas out there to be explored, to commit our dollars or time to explore an idea without a clear, measurable and guaranteed set of outcomes attached. Fear prevents people from doing a lot of things. But our imagination is the single greatest weapon we possess in the fight against thinking that we're inadequate, or unable to make a difference.

Our imagination is what helps us draw the roadmap, build the vehicle, and fuel our movement into the future.

We all believe that change is needed, that there are issues and causes that deserve our attention, areas in our life that could be improved, and products (or whatever you want to call them) that would improve our experiences. We have become too focused on maintaining the status quo, making profit, and optimizing at the expensive of dreaming, inventing and pushing forward.

The Imagination Gap is what is holding us back, preventing us from thinking beyond what we know and can prove — and its long past time that we closed the gap.

Challenge: Make Something Out of Seemingly Nothing

Plastic spoons are more than utensils. They can be glued together, melted, and painted to make gorgeous art projects. Plastic spoons can also be turned into DIY projects for home and garden. Using your imagination, you can create just about anything you want out of a plastic spoon — including a unique and thoughtful gift.

To Do: Find the pile of leftover plastic spoons that you tucked away in your kitchen, garage, basement, or wherever extra things get stored in your home. Put your imagination in overdrive and come up with ways to transform those spoons into something other than plain plastic spoons. Then, give what you made away to someone as a gift.

Challenge: Have a Conversation

In-person conversations are sometimes disregarded as dated or old school. But it's not some vestige of a bygone era. Face-to-face is still the manner in which people prefer to communicate, even with all of the technology available. Meeting in person creates a different kind of sensation than speaking on the phone, exchanging text messages, or responding to posts on Facebook. Your brain engages differently and your imagination is applied in new ways.

To Do: Meet a friend for a cup of coffee. Hang around for a few minutes after dropping your kids off at school. Introduce yourself to the person sitting next to you on the bus to work. Whatever your preferred approach is, make time each day to have a conversation with someone you don't speak with on a regular basis — and do it in person.

NOTES

1. Interview with Hannah Scott — July 12, 2016.
2. *Aquinas, Summa Theologiae, 5, 147.*
3. Sidney, P. *An Apology for Poetry*, 1595, http://www.kleal. com/Sidney%20-%20An%20Apology%20For%20Poetry.pdf
4. Sartre, J.-P. *The Imagination*. Routledge, November 12, 2012, p. 115.
5. Bronowski, J. *The Reach of Imagination*. http://www.public. iastate.edu/~bccorey/105%20Folder/The%20Reach%20of% 20Imagine.pdf
6. https://www.psychologytoday.com/blog/the-athletes-way/ 201306/imagination-can-change-perceptions-reality or http:// ki.se/en/news/imagination-can-change-what-we-hear-and-see or http://www.ncbi.nlm.nih.gov/pubmed/23810539? otool=karolib&tool=karolinska
7. Berger, C.C. & Ehrsson, H.H. (2013). Mental imagery changes multisensory perception. *Current Biology*, 23(14), 1367–1372. doi:10.1016/j.cub.2013.06.012. http://www.ncbi.nlm.nih.gov/ pubmed/23810539?otool=karolib&tool=karolinska
8. http://www.nytimes.com/2013/05/21/science/mit-scholars-1949-essay-on-machine-age-is-found.html
9. Cybernetics: Or Control and Communication in the Animal and the Machine. Paris (Hermann & Cie) & Cambridge, MA (MIT Press). ISBN 978-0-262-73009-9; 1948, 2nd revised ed., 1961.
10. Volume I of the Proceedings of the Second International Symposium: National Security & National Competitiveness: Open Source Solutions Proceedings, 1993. http://www.signalde-sign.net/Age%20of%20Imagination.pdf

11. Based on information provided by Rita J. King — July 17, 2016. King, R.J. *Our Vision for Sustainable Culture in the Imagination Age*. Essay for Paris, 2008.
12. http://www.newyorker.com/magazine/2014/06/23/the-disruption-machine
13. Land, G. & Jarman, B. *Breakpoint and Beyond: Mastering the Future Today*, 1992.

The Imagination
Gap

*As a society, we don't recognize or embrace the critical role of imagina-
tion. It is very difficult for people to understand things they have not
experienced, and without being able to use and apply imagination to its
fullest, we have become paralyzed. This chapter introduces and explains
the Imagination Gap and outlines the specific steps that need to be taken
to unleash and apply our imagination.*

Imagine if ...
　　... every eligible person in the United States — 100% — showed
up at their polling place on the first Tuesday after the first
Monday in November and cast a vote.
　　... nobody was ever forced to flee their homes because of violence and persecution, and that those who have been displaced
could return home safely and resume the lives they had to
abandon.
　　... nobody died of coronary artery failure, Malaria, cancer
(of any kind), or any other disease.
　　... instead of commuting to work, taking a trip to the ballpark,
or running an errand at the store using a car, bus, subway or any
other vehicle, you were converted into an energy pattern and then
beamed to your target destination and rematerialized.
　　These are not ridiculous ideas. Political leaders, humanitarian
advocates, medical experts, and science fiction writers have

suggested each of them, in one form or another, in just the past few years. But the prospects of living in a world in which these ideas represent our reality seem improbable, if not impossible.

There are, of course, plenty of once impossible seeming ideas — a cocktail that can fight certain infections in the body, a supercomputer that fits in your pocket, a computer that can beat a human at a game of chess, an African-American elected President of the United States — that have become a reality.

All of these ideas, and countless others, began with imagination. Our history as a society, and the evolution of the human race, has been driven by imagination. And yet, right now, in every facet of our lives — every industry, every country, every community — we face an Imagination Gap. There are new ideas being generated, but not enough of them. There are ambitious ideas about how to design and shape the future, but people are not acting on them.

Without imagination, our progress is limited. This is true for everyone: business/brands, political and advocacy groups, governments, media, nonprofit, and charitable organizations. Few of us are fully prepared for the kind of transformation that is occurring in our society — where everything, from our economy to health to every aspect of the human experience, looks and functions differently than ever before. It is all happening so quickly, that within a decade or two everything will have changed. And then it will change again, just as quickly. Nobody, it seems, is focusing on what could be possible beyond what is happening now, let alone what's next, or could be possible beyond that.

Information is coming at us fast, and change is happening so rapidly. We all feel like we have to work so hard just to keep up, and that prevents us from stepping away, going outside of our current experience, and imagining other possibilities.

Build Scaffolding

Scaffolding is one of the earliest parts of construction used in human history. Sockets in the walls around cave paintings suggest that a scaffold system was used more than 17,000 years ago to aid early humans in composing their cave paintings. Scaffolding was used by the ancient Greeks to help with construction of the Acropolis. The construction of the Egyptian Pyramids, the Inca temples in Machu Pichu, and The Great Wall of China all required scaffolding as well. And today, you will find scaffolding used to support work crews in the construction, maintenance, and repair of buildings, bridges, and all other man-made structures.

Scaffolding also refers to the foundational skills and supports that educators teach students to help them learn more complex skills. While construction scaffolding uses tubes, couplers, and boards to support workers, in education, scaffolding encompasses a range of instructional techniques designed to systematically build on students' existing knowledge as they are learning new skills. For example, show and tell is used to demonstrate to students how things work, instead of relying solely on a verbal explanation. A teacher will also associate new information with existing knowledge by asking students to share their own experiences with a subject and have them relate and connect it to their own lives. Whatever the specific methodology used, the supports are temporary and adjustable, so as students master the assigned tasks, the supports are gradually removed.

Scaffolding can also be used to help encourage people to use and apply their imagination.

Josh Linkner, an author and venture capitalist, believes you must provide proper support in order to successfully encourage people to use their imagination and think beyond their current perspectives and experiences. "You need some systems or structure on which to lean but make sure that it's loose enough that it isn't striking a rigid-type formulaic approach." Providing that support, or scaffolding, can be used to help close the imagination gap by giving people more confidence in their own ability to use and apply their imagination.

Each person's use and application of imagination is unique and should be encouraged. Josh Linkner suggests Jazz provides a model that could be useful. "Jazz musicians aren't necessarily more creative than anybody else," Linkner told me. "It's not like one out of 1,000 people born is someone really special and they become jazz musicians. It's just that the culture of the jazz supports risk taking and has an optimal balance of structure and freedom." It is very common for a group of jazz musicians to perform together for a whole evening without having previously met or practiced with each other. But there is a structure to the music, scaffolding, that each individual musician can use as a basic support for their participation in an ensemble and expand on from there.

Let's break down how this works for Jazz:

First, to start a tune, the musicians agree on a musical key and the bandleader calls a tempo, or speed, by counting them into the tune. In jazz, there is often an introduction either already written as part of the composition or improvised, most commonly on the piano. Then, all the musicians play the written tune together. Depending on the genre of jazz presented, this opening chorus can be played loosely or even boisterously, with three or more horn players weaving lines collectively around the melody as in Dixieland or traditional New Orleans jazz. Or, it can be played in a more subdued way, as in bebop and cool jazz.

However it is presented, that first chorus is called the "head," and it is generally played once.

Next, each musician in turn plays a solo, improvising around the head for a varying period, taking the chord sequence of the tune itself as their blueprint. Respect for the chord structure of the head is crucial for true jazz. Toward the end of their solo improvisation, the musician reduces the intensity of their playing often dropping down the scale and nodding or pointing to signal an invitation to the next musician to make his or her own improvisation.

After all the front line of musicians have each played their solo improvisation, the musicians in the back play their solos. Bass takes a turn then the drums, which sometimes trade musical phrases with each of the front line. The band operates as an interdependent team.

Every performance is different. For example, not everyone wants to take a solo, nor do they have to — a musician can signal they are passing by looking to the next musician in turn. Through all these changes, the rhythm section keeps the music driving forward in time. When the solos are complete, the band plays the head again, that's the out head or last chorus. There may also be a special ending, written or improvised. To signal the last chorus, the band leader may raise his hand.

Linkner notes that the scaffolding that supports the jazz musicians also gives them the ability to contribute to the performance in novel ways. "If you're playing jazz, and you play it safe — just doing what you know is going to work — you will pretty much get laughed off the stage. But if you take a risk and you screw something up and you play a honk or a bad note you just play it twice more, you just call it art. Everything is cool. That's the culture of jazz." That culture of experimentation and exploration doesn't exist in business, politics, academia, or any other sector — and there is a lot about how jazz functions, and uses scaffolding, that others could benefit from learning.

Do You Have Sheet Music on This Stuff?

In the final scene of the movie *Dirty Dancing*, Johnny Castle (played by Patrick Swayze), Baby (played by Jennifer Grey), and an ensemble of dancers crash the annual end-of-summer performance at Kellerman's, the resort in the Catskills Mountains that serves as the setting for the film. Johnny has returned to do the last dance of the season (as is tradition), and delivers his famous line, "Nobody puts Baby in the corner" before leading Baby onstage to perform the now-iconic routine set to the song "(I've Had) The Time of My Life" by Bill Medley.

While seemingly everyone is quickly consumed by the moment, and motivated to join in the dancing, the movie cuts to the resort director, watching from the side of the stage. He turns to one of Johnny's crew and asks, "do you have sheet music on this stuff?" The moment embodies a key disconnect between the established forces in our society and those who seek to push and evolve how we live. And it shows how challenging it is for people who are set in their ways to use their imagination to explore new ideas.

We become dependent on what is known, comfortable, and easily repeatable — music that can be written down, practiced, perfected, and performed. But it is the live performance or the unplanned flourish that shows the true genius of the musician and most excites the audience. It is music that pushes new boundaries or is improvised such as with jazz that helps push music forward.

Imagination is not about producing a specific outcome and doesn't respond to a set approach. When considering the best ways to encourage people to think differently, structure can be important, but too much structure is limiting. In some cases structure changes the very nature of the challenge, from considering every possible option to a limited set that addresses a specific need. A lack of structure isn't constructive either.

A lot of music is created so that it can only be performed in one specific way. Jazz is more fluid and dynamic by design. In any form of music, as with imagination and its byproducts, there are a number of different types of structures that can be considered. Charles Mingus, one of most important figures in 20th century American music, famously said "You cannot improvise on nothin' man. You gotta improvise on somethin." That something Mingus was referring to is a mixture of structure and flexibility. Musicians improve using an appropriate balance between control and autonomy. For music, the structure comes in the tempo while the flexibility comes from different chord progressions or key signatures that can be applied to any other situation. The structure exists so that the group of musicians can all find some common ground, but then also have the freedom to play the tunes that they conceive of in their imagination.

I played a lot of instruments growing up. Starting in elementary school, I was enrolled in both piano and violin lessons. Up through middle school, I attempted to learn, and eventually master the tuba, trombone, and trumpet in the hopes of becoming a member of the marching band. I played triangle in my school orchestra and put a drum set in our basement so I could start a rock band. With every instrument I took lessons, I practiced, I performed in concerts — and ultimately I stopped playing.

Musicians prepare for years to achieve technical proficiency and then continually practice even after they attain it. They are constantly improving their skills, and building new musical capabilities. They remain focused on fundamentals and strive to improve every note they play. For some musicians, this leads to complete mastery of their craft — and affords them opportunities to play the most challenging musical compositions. That mastery can serve as the scaffolding that then invites the musician to apply their imagination and create their own music.

I washed out as a musician. I didn't survive the learning portion and, thus, never achieved the mastery that would allow me to fully explore my musical imagination. Mark Oppenheimer, an author who focuses on the interaction between belief/religion and popular culture, would argue that washing out was not entirely my fault.

Oppenheimer believes that children should not be forced to take music lessons. In an article in "The New Republic," he wrote that our habit of encouraging kids to take music lessons made sense in the past — but doesn't any longer.

> Before the twentieth century, there was a good reason for anyone to study music: If you couldn't make the music yourself, then you would rarely hear it. Before the radio and the phonograph, any music in the house was produced by the family itself. So it made sense to play fiddle, piano, jug, whatever. And before urbanization and the automobile, most people did not have easy, regular access to concerts. Of course, small-town people could come together for occasional concerts, to play together or to hear local troupes or traveling bands. Growing up in the sticks, you still might see Shakespeare performed, and a touring opera company could bring you Mozart. But very infrequently. If music was to be a part of your daily life, it had to be homemade.[1]

Oppenheimer doesn't completely oppose the idea of music lessons, but does believe that emphasizing repetition and rote playing does more harm than good when it comes to the music skills that ultimately spark our imagination. "The classes are not a bad thing. Studying music or dance over a long time teaches perseverance and can build self-confidence," he writes. "But then again, studying *anything* over a long time teaches perseverance and can build self-confidence. There is no special virtue in knowing how to play the violin, unless you have a special gift for the violin. Otherwise, you're learning the same valuable lessons that you'd get from karate class, or from badminton. Or from endless hours of foosball."

He also acknowledges that, "there are benefits to having a society where more people are engaged with the arts, so even if music instruction doesn't make you a better mathematician or a better athlete, even if it only gives you the enjoyment of music, that is a good thing." But he warns, "if the approach we take to learning music ultimately undermines our capacity to utilize our imagination in other ways, the negatives outweigh the positives for sure."

There are plenty of people who receive formal music training, put in the required work to practice and refine their skills, and are successful. My inability to master an instrument, or stay committed to playing music, was not because of lack of interest or even capability (although in the case of the trombone, the length of the slide was greater than the reach of my arms, so it was almost impossible to play some notes). My musical career also wasn't doomed due to a lack of practice. I put in my time. To this day, I love music so much that when I attend a concert, or just hear my daughter play something on the piano, I yearn to be able to play, write, and perform music.

I wasn't given the opportunity to really play music. I wasn't encouraged to let my musical imagination run wild, nor pursue the musical ideas that I generated. Throughout my time learning to read notes and express sounds through various instruments, whether I was in private lessons or part of a group class, in school or elsewhere, I was repeatedly told I must follow a strict regimen. As a music student, I was only given the chance to play other people's music. The set list was also provided for me. Not only was I instructed to practice what was on the page, when I dared to improvise, I was told to stop. My musical imagination slowly and steadily diminished.

Music, like every other art, cannot be played outside the bounds of what you know. When you watch great musicians, they make their extraordinary talents appear effortless. But, like others, their minds have been developed to a point that they can picture and play in a flash. Their imagination is what provides the fuel for their expression.

The Think System

In Meredith Wilson's musical, *The Music Man* Professor Harold Hill, a traveling salesman and apparent con man, arrives in River City, Iowa, and convinces the locals to start a band, complete with shiny new instruments and uniforms. While everyone awaits the arrival of the provisions they have ordered, Professor Hill pretends to teach River City's children to play music using what he calls the "Think System." The Think System does not require the use an instrument. Instead, Professor Hill encourages the kids in the band to repeatedly verbalize the melody of Beethoven's Minuet in G (Lad-di-da-di-da-di-da-di-dah ...).

The parents of River City become convinced they are the unwilling victims of a scam and a group of angry townsfolk assemble to tar and feather Professor Hill. But the band, in hopes of saving Professor Hill, assembles to play Minuet in G — putting into practice what they have learned using the Think Method. While many of the notes hit the wrong key, the kids have in fact transformed into a band. They sound pretty awful, but the parents and townspeople still hear something special — thanks in large part to their imagination.

Professor Hill's Think System may have been part of a scam — he hoped to leave town before anyone figured it out — but, the concept of visual imaging has validity, in music and beyond. Visual imaging is one of the central functions of our imagination. Like with show and tell in education, and structured chords in jazz, it's a form of scaffolding that can help people to learn how to play an instrument, and much more.

Visual imaging is an example of how we use our imagination, allowing a musician to hear or see the notes to be played, even before any audible sound emerges. It is what allows us each to round out our understanding of reality when we don't have all the knowledge or direct experience we need to know something for sure. When we are unable, or unwilling, to believe that something we haven't experienced directly — and cannot prove definitively — is real, that is an example of the imagination gap. The "Think System" isn't (entirely) a scam dreamed up by Professor Harold Hill; it's an example of our imagination at work.

Science without the Experimentation

It would be easy — and in fact it is quite common — for imagination to be associated solely with arts and creative pursuits. But that would diminish the valuable role that imagination plays in every sector of our society.

Science relies on the use and application of imagination to prompt new questions and uncover breakthrough interpretations of new or unexpected findings. The role that science plays in exploring and ultimately proving new theories about our universe is possible because a basic structure exists to govern the conduct of science — namely, The Scientific Method.

The Scientific Method has been the subject of intense and recurring debate throughout the history of science. Different philosophers and scientists, from Aristotle to Descartes to Isaac Newton to Richard Feynman, have all offered their own variation on the most appropriate way to determine what is provable, verifiable, and appropriate in our quest to understand the natural world. In recent years, as new research methodologies and sources of data have become available, the questions about whether a universal methodology can be applied have surfaced again, and with further advancements, such debates will likely continue.

The basic components of the Scientific Method demand that a scientific experiment must include a series of steps, including:

— Determining the question or a problem;

— Collecting all the facts about the problem;

— Proposing a theory or possible explanation (a hypothesis);

— Testing the theory with an experiment;

— Repeating the experiment to test if it will always be true.

If those steps are followed, and the hypothesis proves to be always true, it becomes scientific law. If it doesn't, it is rejected, and you start over. As long as those steps are followed, a standard exists and the experimentation can be reviewed and shared.

But everything else — beyond the basic structure of the scientific method — not only is open to the imagination of the scientists, but also demands their use and application of imagination in order to be worthwhile. From Einstein's theory of relativity to the present day discussion of climate change, the absence of certainty fuels the imagination of scientists and drives endless discussion and experimentation.

The most important scientific theories and discoveries began as ideas — hypotheses that were imagined by someone then proven through experimentation. Take Galileo, Newton, and Einstein as examples, — their genius was as much a product of imagination as it is procedure. The determination of the questions, the hypotheses they develop, the tests they run — and in some cases, the meaning of the results — are all the result of their capacity, and willingness, to use and apply their imagination.

Every day, in the field and in the lab, scientists use and apply their imaginations to the job of wondering, noticing, questioning, investigating, and making sense of the natural world. They can't rely solely on their imagination — they draw on previous knowledge and continuously integrate the results of their ongoing experimentation. They are also subject to secondary or tertiary review of their work by peers.

Ideas begin in the imagination, but become real and provable through adherence to scientific method. Our willingness and ability to integrate imagination into the scientific method is a model for how we might consider ways to use and apply our imagination beyond science as well.

Imagine Everything; Don't Decide Anything (Yet)

The practical examples of using one's imagination includes creating mental images, exploring counterfactual conjecture, entertaining alternative pasts, daydreaming, fantasizing, pretending, and simulating other people's experiences, mental rehearsal, and creating or inventing things that haven't existed before. What connects all of those different outputs is that they embrace "anything is possible." For that to work, however, you have to truly believe that anything is possible and not let logic or evidence influence your thinking and curb your imagination.

We try to use our knowledge to prove or disprove ideas — but often end up passing judgment before something is able to be considered. Think about it: just because something is true doesn't mean it can be proved. And just because something can be proved doesn't mean it's true. As Jonah Lehrer wrote in his book *Proust Was a Neuroscientist*:

> Every brilliant experiment, like every great work of art, starts with an act of imagination. Unfortunately, our current culture subscribes to a very narrow definition of truth. If something can't be quantified and calculated, then it can't be true. Because this strict scientific approach has explained so much, we assume that it can explain everything. But every method, even the experimental method, has limits. Take the human mind. Scientists describe our brain in terms of its physical details; they say we are nothing but a loom of electrical cells and synaptic spaces. What science forgets is that this isn't how we experience the world. (We feel like

the ghost, not like the machine.) It is ironic but true: the one reality science cannot reduce is the only reality we will ever know. This is why we need art. By expressing our actual experience, the artist reminds us that our science is incomplete, that no map of matter will ever explain the immateriality of our consciousness.[2]

All we accomplish by pre-deciding something is eliminate options that might be worth pursuing later. Knowing something about how the world works also suggest we know the reasons the world does not operate in some other way. But, we don't know why one thing happened or didn't, not with any certainty. We use our imagination to fill in the blanks and create a version of reality that makes sense to us. We not only become numb to the possibilities of something new, but we also actively suppress ideas that challenge what we have been told is reasonable.

Instead of trying to keep new ideas from forming, we should be training our brains to constantly put new ideas together and share them widely. We should prime our brain into thinking in a way that is more imaginative. You can try to tell yourself to be more imaginative, but it won't work. The better option by far is to change what your brain believes it is doing.

The idea of priming is simple: you can train a person's brain to do certain things without directing a specific, or even conscious, action. Take one of the most famous experiments demonstrating the power of priming: Two groups of people were given the task of unscrambling some sentences. One group's sentences included words like wrinkles, Florida, and shuffleboard. What those sentences were meant to do was to evoke an image of elderly people and old age. That's the priming. The actual experiment happened when people were asked to walk down the hall to a different room for the second part of the experiment. The dependent variable was how fast they walked. People who were primed to think about old age overwhelmingly went slower.

Darya Zabelina, a cognitive researcher, told me about another experiment conducted by psychologist Michael Robinson to test the effects of priming on imagination and creative thinking.

Robinson randomly assigned a few hundred undergraduates to two different groups. The first group was given the following instructions: "You are 7 years old, and school is canceled. You have the entire day to yourself. What would you do? Where would you go? Who would you see?" The second group was given the exact same instructions, without the guidance regarding age. As a result, the second group of students didn't imagine themselves as seven year olds. After writing for 10 minutes, the students were then given various tests — they were asked to invent alternative uses for an old car tire, or to list the things you could do with a brick. The students who imagined themselves as young kids scored far higher on the creative tasks, coming up with twice as many ideas as the control group.

In one summary of the report, Robinson explains: "When you play a role of an adult, you take yourself and life very seriously. Spontaneity, lightheartedness, and joy are not part of that role."[3] His results show that we are able to tap into our imagination, even if it has been diminished by criticism or lack of use over time. We just have to pretend we're a little kid.

Have Faith in Your Imagination

How do you capture the public's imagination? As we have discussed, each of our imaginations is unique, and our experience informs the ideas we have, as well as our willingness to embrace others' way of seeing things. There are very few elements of our lives where imagination can flourish and not be influenced by the desire to measure and quantify its output. The most notable of these is faith.

Macky Alston, a documentary filmmaker and organizer who teaches at Union Theological Seminary in New York, has been wrestling with this challenge throughout his career. His research has explored the decline of organized social activism in the digital age and the declining influence that faith and religious organizations have on social justice issues. He and his colleagues have tried to determine whether you can recapture the public's imagination on social issues, and if so, what steps need to be taken. He told me "in the last ten years I have media-trained 5,000 leaders of faith and moral courage to figure out how to do that better through the media, how to capture the public imagination better through story, through ravishing public speech, through speaking to people's hearts in a seven second sound bite." He summarized his approach:

> I effectively help people come to voice and to say what they believe to be true in the most evocative, powerful, story-based, heartbreaking form. I focus on what it means to love them, to believe in them — from their perspective. And when I do that they come out of their cave or shell and vulnerably share their most beautiful realities, and it's always fabulous. It's always fabulous.

Alston believes that all people have huge capacity for imagination, but his research reveals some of the challenges when trying to bring it to the surface. His experience affirms that we are most imaginative when we are kids, but also cautions that "there is a correlation between how we are treated and nurtured and how imaginative we are."

He cited the parallel example of how many perceive faith, and participate in organized religion, as areas within our society where imagination and belief are supposed to be celebrated. You are supposed to be able to believe what you believe. But in practice, organized faith and the business of religion in modern times present a very different reality. He said that notion that houses of worship or churches or religions are places where imagination is free to flourish is not entirely accurate — and that often faith and religion are used to influence what people think, and limit the bounds of what people are encouraged to believe. Alston analogized this to "when kids are oppressed, beaten, or told are worthless," noting that in those situations, "their imaginations aren't flourishing."

Over and over again in his work, Alston has seen the effects of people growing up in a culture that does not embrace imagination. He explains "Grownups are so judged and self-critical, are so terrified of losing our jobs and of being ostracized in our social circles, that we do almost anything, post-adolescence, to not rock the boat. We want to conform. We want to be popular. We want to get a raise. We want to get ahead. We watch what works and we replicate it." And drawing an even clearer distinction between innovation and imagination, he said "Innovation often is a product of privilege and the innovators often are the ones who feel like they don't have the same amount to lose that others do. Or they have nothing to lose in another regard where they have been so pushed up against the wall by life that they say, "Fuck it," you know? "I will choose life over death because I've tasted death and I don't like it."

Challenges to Applying Imagination

There are opportunities to use and apply imagination every day, in business and the arts, politics and education, science, religion, and more. Typically, if imagination is recognized and invited into our approach, it is at the beginning of the process — when people are planning and discussing what might be possible. At the beginning, there is greater interest and willingness to consider different ideas. But as milestones are achieved and details become fixed, it becomes more challenging to find a place for imagination.

Jake Siewert has worked at the highest level of politics, and with the leaders of major corporations. He now heads corporate communications for Goldman Sachs. Siewert says one of the biggest challenges facing banks — as well as other large, institutional type organizations — is the need to distinguish themselves from their competitors. He believes that having the ability to use and apply one's imagination is an important part of figuring that out.

> Every bank that comes in to advise a client – whether the client is a stodgy old corporation in the mining and metals industry like I used to work at, or a cutting edge hedge fund that's trying to figure out how to do a little

bit better than their competitors – every bank has the ability to tell them what's going on in the world. "Here's what's happened in the markets over the last six months. Here's what it looks like is happening right now." Everyone has competent people who can run the numbers and look at the price of aluminum, or electricity, or whatever the key factors are that affect a particular industry.

At Goldman Sachs, we make an effort to think well beyond the present. "Here's your industry; here's what's going on in your industry; here's the financials, such as they are. But let's look at what's going on in the world and look at what's happening in geopolitics and start thinking around the corner." When you're thinking about your firm and making big decisions about what the future is going to look like, you want someone who's going to try to help you think around the corner. And that takes imagination because that isn't just gleaned from looking at the stats about the aluminum cycle price.

Siewert suggests that the imagination gap exists because of our tendency to overvalue the present. "When you're in the moment, you can't imagine that something will ever be any other way. But you have to remind yourself that you're going to feel exactly that same way when it's very different. The overvaluing of the present is particularly endemic if you trade in the markets all day."

Jason Rosenkrantz, a multimedia storyteller, agrees and argues that the reason so many industries are focused on the present is because that is how people are taught, from an early age, to approach their work. "Imagination isn't just silenced, its devalued by society and especially by the school system. The public school system was set up to supply a workforce during the industrial revolution. It wasn't set up with the purpose of creating the most capable problem solvers," he argues.

The resulting structure of our education system — and the corporate and institutional structures that rely on our education system to produce their employees — relies heavily on testing to determine which students are performing best. As a result, we approach the task of teaching people — regardless of age — toward optimizing performance on those tests. That is fine if the challenges facing each of us, or the planet more broadly for example, can be addressed in a way that mirrors that style of learning. In most cases it does not. Education and employment that, perhaps unintentionally, celebrates standardization sends a clear message that imagination is not a valuable attribute.

"Today, we really need as many creative problem solvers as possible. That's much more valuable to us than just creating the human equivalent of robots," Rosenkrantz explains. Unfortunately, that hasn't stopped the creative thinking from getting tamped down or getting silenced. And when that gets suppressed as a kid, you forget about it. You're taught that there's no value in it. You're taught that you should be doing X, Y and Z because that's what the system demands and that's what will lead to successful lives.

The tendency to do something the way it's always been done is very powerful. "Even in places that pride themselves on doing things differently, you will still hear people say 'Well we've always done it this way,'" says Jake Siewert.

One Size Doesn't Fit All

We are not all Galileo, Newton, or Einstein. We are not Mozart, John Coltrane, or even Professor Harold Hill. We are, however, all unique and our imaginations are powered and influenced by our individual experiences and the context of our lives. There are people whose imagination is cultivated and fostered all the time. There are other people who are given direct orders or narrow parameters within which to operate and are only able to use and apply their imagination in limited cases, if at all. But, everybody has an imagination. We need to use our imaginations to understand that there is an imagination gap. We need to use our imaginations to address the imagination gap. So we must be willing to use and apply our imagination. And it is equally important to recognize the different ways that imagination takes shape for every individual. We cannot pass judgment or dismiss anyone's capacity for imagination under any circumstance.

The Imagination Gap exists because the structures and ways that we function as a society fail to recognize the value and potential that imagination offers. We've created structures to protect the people who are already considered creative or the handful of ideas that qualify as bold and novel. Consistent with how our society has advanced — from the industrial age, through the information age and beyond, there has been a massive effort to streamline or operationalize creativity and innovation. Those systems and structures have undermined our individual and collective interest in imagination. They created the Imagination Gap and they continue to perpetuate its damaging impact.

We have to change the way we think and talk about imagination. We have to unbuild the structures that are in place that actively block imagination from being used, applied, and embraced. Ultimately, we have to close the Imagination Gap.

The gap is between the boundless potential that imagination creates — all the ideas, insights, and options that we fail to consider, don't think are possible, and haven't begun to pursue — and the structured, consumer-focused world in which we live. We have done so much to systematize and monetize the idea of creativity, and innovation, that we have made it nearly impossible to use and apply our imagination in the ways that are most exciting, and have the most potential to create dramatic and long-lasting change.

Challenge: Be Surprised

Comedy is a surprise of expectation. Our expectations are met with something exaggerated and odd. Surprise is the key to successful humor — and also a trigger of imagination. You have to go into things just to do them, without an agenda, without knowledge of what will happen, and without expectations of how things might unfold. When you do that, you open yourself up to any number of possibilities.

To Do: Don't Google a person before you meet them. Don't read a review of the movie you are going to see before you go to see it. Don't schedule every minute of your day with meetings and events. Just get started and be surprised by what happens.

Challenge: Look at the Clouds

The Cloud Appreciation Society has a manifesto that reads, in part: "WE BELIEVE that clouds are unjustly maligned and that life would be immeasurably poorer without them. We think that they are Nature's poetry, and the most egalitarian of her displays, since everyone can have a fantastic view of them ... We believe that clouds are for dreamers and their contemplation benefits the soul. Indeed, all who consider the shapes they see in them will save money on psychoanalysis bills." Maybe they know something most people don't.

To Do: Look at the clouds. What do you see?

NOTES

1. https://newrepublic.com/article/114733/stop-forcing-your-kids-learn-musical-instrument
2. Lehrer, J. *Proust Was a Neuroscientist*. Houghton Mifflin, 2007, p. xii.
3. https://www.psychologytoday.com/files/attachments/34246/zabelina-robinson-2010a.pdf

The Knowledge and ▶3 Leadership Crises

Two of the key factors that contribute to the Imagination Gap are a lack of knowledge and the absence of true leadership across our society. Our brains are designed to pay attention to specific signals and interests that are most acute in our lives. We make sense of the world by connecting the experiences that are familiar to the unknown. Imagination serves as a bridge. But when we lack knowledge, or clarity, we too often gravitate toward things we like, or are familiar with — even if they are not relevant — and repeat behaviors we have taken before.

Imagination can be our vehicle to escape from current reality. Using our imagination, we can transport ourselves to anywhere we want, real or make-believe, as well as create new things that the world has never seen. Imagination is also an essential tool that we can use to learn about the world in which we live today — whether we're just thinking around the corner, aiming to understand other people, or figuring out whether two puzzle pieces fit together.

How far we allow our imagination to explore, and how we apply what we dream up, is directly tied to how much we know. Our ability to embrace new, different ideas that emerge from our imagination is linked to our willingness to consider the possibility that there are things in the world that we don't yet know. We must accept that we don't know everything. We also must be willing to embrace imagination as a tool in our learning process — and be careful not to dismiss the concepts that we can't prove, or defend, as ridiculous fantasy. Our imagination, if we follow through and apply it in the right ways, is simply a foreshadowing of what we don't know yet.

Our imagination is powered, in part, by what we know and what we have experienced. All the inputs from your life — the facts you collected from going to school or reading a book, the memories you formed on a vacation or business trip, the conversation you overheard while walking down the street — combine and recombine to form the ingredients that fuel your imagination.

We all possess an unlimited capacity to use our imagination. But it is equally important that what emerges from the darkest and most interesting parts of our brain is also given a chance to be shared with others. Our ideas are compelling, but they can neither inspire nor inform others, nor ever become a reality, if they remain only in our heads. Our ability to express what we believe has some limitations — not because of laws (we can say what we believe to be true and our speech is protected) or even for practical reasons (we can post, share, and promote information across numerous channels with a single click). Instead, the imagination gap exists because we are too often told, in words and deeds, that imagination has no value. The imagination gap exists because we believe that we must follow the people, and the actions, that have proven to be successful before.

To change that we need more people to not just believe, but also advocate for the value that imagination provides. We need teachers and politicians, business and civic leaders to encourage us to work toward a future that is beyond what we know and can appreciate. We also need our parents and friends, colleagues and fellow community members to be encouraging if, or when, we share our ideas for what might be possible. We all share some responsibility for closing the imagination gap. We all have an obligation to lead in this important discussion. We will all benefit when more people to stand up and speak out, leading the way so that everyone is empowered to show our imagination in full.

Seeing Around the Corner

Some of what we imagine is entirely new — unrecognizable from our current reality. The product is pure fantasy, not because the idea is unattainable, but because it's not based on our current experiences. Let's say you imagine the life of an alien creature on a far-away planet and that unfamiliar being is spending time watching (the alien version of) a sit-com on (the alien version of) a TV, or they are completing a household chore with (the alien version of) a vacuum. While you have created a new reality out of your imagination, you have also mixed in elements of your own current experiences. The alien is new, but their version of a television show or a ShopVac is based on the ones you know exist. They are all products of your imagination, but in different ways.

The ability to know something before it happens, before it becomes real, would certainly have practical value. This is not about picking the winning lottery numbers or predicting the weather. Imagination helps to create a picture of the future that you can use to make informed choices about how to act. The images that form in your imagination help shape your day-to-day behaviors in ways you probably take for granted. But they are important. For example, they help to keep you alive.

Timothy Williamson, a Professor of Logic at Oxford University and a Fellow of the British Academy and a Foreign Honorary Member of the American Academy of Arts and Sciences, explained in an op-ed for the *New York Times* that reality-based imagination has survival value, and that "by enabling you to imagine all sorts of scenarios, it alerts you to dangers and opportunities." In other words, it keeps you from making the worst possible mistakes. He wrote:

> You come across a cave. You imagine wintering there with a warm fire — opportunity. You imagine a bear waking up inside — danger. Having imagined possibilities, you can take account of them in contingency planning. If a bear is in the cave, how do you deal with it? If you winter there, what do you do for food and drink?

Answering those questions involves more imagining, which must be reality-directed.

Of course, you can imagine kissing the angry bear as it emerges from the cave so that it becomes your life-long friend and brings you all the food and drink you need. Better not to rely on such fantasies. Instead, let your imaginings develop in ways more informed by your knowledge of how things really happen.[1]

The key, Williamson suggests, is in how we balance what we know and what we imagine as possible. Without the ability to imagine new things beyond what we have seen or experience first-hand, and accept what we imagine as plausible, it becomes difficult to advance.

We learn through our experiences — not just directly, but from our observation how others act, and the impact that actions have on others. We make sense of how to behave and what choices not to make often first from making mistakes. And we should hope that the lessons learned through adversity are transferrable to many different situations, so that we don't have to learn everything the hard way. We benefit from using our imagination because it alleviates the need to have direct evidence ourselves to serve as proof.

We apply our imagination in this way on various levels. First, on an individual level, we supplement our own personal, first-hand experiences with ones that we imagine. This allows us to recognize the danger of touching a hot stove without ever having to sustain a burn ourselves or appreciate the benefits of looking both ways when crossing the street while never having to walk in front of a moving vehicle. Second, our imagination contributes to how we act as a community by influencing our social norms. For example, by imagining the hurt and pain that people endure, we can condemn discrimination without ever having to be on the receiving end of any bad acts. Similarly, we can support the formation of laws or policy without any direct impact on our lives (e.g., supporting gay marriage without knowing a same-sex couple).

There are limitations to how much we can each experience directly — and real consequences that result from making mistakes. If we insisted on personal, hands-on experience for everything, we would not have achieved many of the scientific discoveries or technological advancements we have (because so many of them are built on top of things that were built and made available before). We also would not evolve as a species, because inability to leap ahead, skipping over steps that others had already confirmed through their experience, would hold us back. As Ursula Le Guin wrote: "We will not know our own injustice if we cannot imagine justice. We will not be free if we do not imagine freedom. We cannot demand that anyone try to attain justice and freedom who has not had a chance to imagine them as attainable."[2]

Consider, for example, how our earliest human ancestors used their imagination to consider what might be happening to their friends who weren't returning when venturing outside of their cave — and adapted as a result. Without imagination, one Neanderthal after another would have gone out of their cave in search of food, or even just to explore, only to find himself or herself on the losing end of an interaction with a prehistoric animal. There wouldn't be human society at all without imagination and we wouldn't be here talking about this. And for each of us, imagination provides sufficient justification to not try to kiss that bear. Imagination is one of the vehicles we use to bridge between what we know and have experienced, and what might be possible in the future.

The Value of Knowledge is Changing

Once we collect and store information we call that knowledge. While there is no single definition that encompasses all its many attributes, we know that the facts, information, and skills acquired through our experiences and education are classified as knowledge. There is practical knowledge (things we can do) and theoretical knowledge (things we know but haven't experienced). We can obtain knowledge directly, but we also file things under knowledge when we have seen or heard them from others, or we accept that there is broad agreement about something (which can also lead to things becoming fact that are anything but true). Ultimately, the most important consideration when it comes to knowledge is this: when we know something we don't need to revisit or experience again (at least until we find out that the context has changed and what we know has to be reconsidered. Let's come back to that later). Knowledge is supposed to be fixed. It is different than emotion or belief, because knowledge — once ingrained — is supposed to never change. Once we know something, it is essentially hard wired into our brain.

Throughout human history, from the earliest philosophers to today's Jeopardy champions, we celebrate people who possess the greatest amount of knowledge. That includes people who travel to far-flung places (and presumably through that experience learn amazing new things), as well as those who possess the greatest skill when it comes to memorizing and recalling information. In every setting, from the playground to the boardroom, the people who demonstrate that they have the greatest amount of knowledge, about a particular subject or command of a particular discipline, are afforded a certain status.

Having earned that status, those with the most knowledge — or smartest people — are often put on a path that benefits them in other ways. The students with the highest grade point average (GPA) in high school are more likely to get accepted to the best colleges. Employers use academic performance, and test scores, to determine which candidates are most likely to succeed if hired. A person who has worked in a company the longest, and has the benefit of knowing the most about how that organization functions, are often elevated to senior roles.

Knowledge is indeed a powerful asset — but only truly valuable when applied in the proper context. The person can recite the opening passages of The Canterbury Tales is, without question, very smart. But how will that knowledge help them to survive when stranded on a desert island, or staring down a group of potential funders in hopes of receiving investment in a new startup venture? When a market has been disrupted and a company has no choice but to transform from a traditional manufacturer to a cutting-edge digital enterprise, will the knowledge gained by someone who worked their way up from the assembly line to the C-suite be able to see the challenges that lie ahead?

Nobody knows how to do everything, and none of us are born with knowledge of how to do anything. We are, in the words of 17th century philosopher, John Locke, a tabula rasa — or blank slate — with tremendous potential (and a capacity for a big imagination) that can be applied in any number of different ways. Still, we all learn to walk, speak, write (and type), and everything else we need to survive and thrive. Some of what we learn we get through our direct experience, but much of it is also supplemented through the use of our imagination.

In the digital age, our individual access to knowledge is greater than ever — so the usefulness of being able to retain and produce information from memory has diminished. The definition of intelligence is changing. The role of knowledge is being reconsidered. How we teach, and how we learn to prepare for the future, is being challenged. What we know for sure is that we are all connected, not just to each other by technology or shared experience, but through our collective role in contributing to and benefiting from human knowledge. Increasingly, what one person knows, and can contribute to what we all know, is available online. People who have greater experience with a certain subject don't necessarily have an advantage. The greatest value comes from our ability to apply knowledge in the ways that are needed at any given time. And the measure of that value is subjective, ultimately determined by whoever is impacted most.

The Internet is considered as one of the greatest learning tools ever created. But what happens when everyone has his or her own device and the ability to shape their own knowledge experience? How do we know what is true or not, and how to distinguish between fact and imagination? What happens is the value of knowledge changes. Determining what is true becomes more challenging. We each decide whom we trust and what we consider to be useful and valuable knowledge. There is no easy way to compare who knows more than someone else — or whether that is important. And ultimately, there is less interest in the ability to retain information and more attention is paid to figuring out how knowledge can be applied, in the present, and especially with an eye toward the future.

Albert Einstein famously said "Imagination is more important than knowledge. For knowledge is limited to all we now know and understand, while imagination embraces the entire world, and all there ever will be to know and understand."

Failures of Imagination

The National Commission on Terrorist Attacks Upon the United States (also known as the 9–11 Commission) was an independent, bipartisan commission created by the Congress and approved by President George W. Bush in late 2002. It was chartered to prepare a full and complete account of the circumstances surrounding the 9/11 terrorist attacks, including preparedness for and the immediate response to the attacks. The Commission is also mandated to provide recommendations designed to guard against future attacks.

The Commission wrote a report that provided the fullest possible account of the events surrounding 9/11, identified the lessons learned as a result of the attack, and provided actionable recommendations to ensure that such an attack would never happen again. The Executive Summary of the report began as follows:

> At 8:46 on the morning of September 11, 2001, the United States became a nation transformed.
>
> An airliner traveling at hundreds of miles per hour and carrying some 10,000 gallons of jet fuel plowed into the North Tower of the World Trade Center in Lower Manhattan. At 9:03, a second airliner hit the South Tower. Fire and smoke billowed upward. Steel, glass, ash, and bodies fell below. The Twin Towers, where up to 50,000 people worked each day, both collapsed less than 90 minutes later.

At 9:37 that same morning, a third airliner slammed into the western face of the Pentagon. At 10:03, a fourth airliner crashed in a field in southern Pennsylvania. It had been aimed at the United States Capitol or the White House, and was forced down by heroic passengers armed with the knowledge that America was under attack.

More than 2,600 people died at the World Trade Center; 125 died at the Pentagon; 256 died on the four planes. The death toll surpassed that at Pearl Harbor in December 1941.[3]

The report criticized government officials for not recognizing the possibility that terrorists might fly a plane into the World Trade Center. Ultimately, the Commission concluded that the attacks were the result of failures across the government — including policy, capabilities, and management. "The most important failure," the report cited, however "was one of imagination."

The Commission added, "We do not believe leaders understood the gravity of the threat."

It is not clear from the Commission's findings that anyone, other than the terrorists themselves, had ever even considered such a highly complex attack. And even if all of the systems in place had operated perfectly, the Commission concluded that some sort of attack probably still would have occurred, because there were too many weaknesses to protect against perfectly. Of course, it is common for large institutions — such as the government or the security apparatus for the United States — to prioritize facts and actionable intelligence, leaving little room for imagination to help fill in the gaps. "Every day you spend in a windowless office inside some government institution, your ability to dream big, in many respects, is killed off," Alec Ross told me.[4]

Ross is the former head of Innovation at the State Department and author of *Industries of the Future*, a book that explores the future business and societal challenges facing the planet and how best to address them. "If you look at an issue like clean energy,

I don't think any sort of incremental approach is going to get us where we need to be. What do I think we need? I think we need a conceptual breakthrough that would absolutely be laughed at by most of today's scientists." He suggested that it is not very common for institution to allow their people to develop that kind of thinking, to build frameworks around it, or to advocate for those types of imagination-driven projects. "I think that we're going to need really free spirits to light the path for us." That won't happen, Ross suggests, as long as people don't recognize the possibility that threats — especially those beyond their personal knowledge or experience — might occur.

Daniel Pink, author of several books, including *A Whole New Mind*, made a similar point back in 2006, suggesting during an interview with *Forbes Magazine* that when massive economic shifts occur, people are terrible at foreseeing what's next. As late as 2006, Pink noted, economists were still arguing that manufacturing was required as a foundation for a strong economy. No one "envisioned search-engine optimizers or web designers or executive coaches or nanotechnologists." Pink predicted an "imagination economy" where the future will bring "industries we can't imagine and jobs which we lack the vocabulary to describe."[5] At the time, his comments were either overlooked or dismissed. Fast forward a decade and its very clear that Pink was right on the mark.

What causes these failures of imagination? Like Alec Ross, Pink says "when we're cabined in the present, we suffer from a certain poverty of imagination. We massively underestimate human ingenuity and resilience." He argues it takes a leap of faith to accept the possibility of something we have not yet experienced. A leap of faith, of course, is just another way to describe what happens when you are using and applying your imagination. A leap of faith is not some intellectual exercise, it is you being open to the prospect of something happening in the future balanced with existing knowledge.

Take for example what happened on 9/11 after the first planes struck the World Trade Center. Security officials quickly recognized that other aircrafts might also be used to attack, and imagining how that type of situation might unfold, scrambled military jets to intercept any suspicious aircrafts and called for the grounding of all commercial flights. In the days and weeks that followed, the imaginations of people went wild and nearly everything that wasn't proven to be harmless was labeled as a potential threat and investigated thoroughly.

We value knowledge most and there is no other evidence to suggest otherwise. We are comfortable with what we have proven to be true in the past when there is no reason to believe the future will present a new set of challenges. But the future always presents new challenges. And we often find ourselves slow to recognize or respond to changes until it's too late. We are more willing to experiment and explore — and to draw on our imagination — when there are signs that indicate something isn't working, or what we knew to be true is no longer true. If a product still sells and generates profit for a company — why stop? If the message a nonprofit organization is promoting is still motivating people to donate or volunteer, why change strategies?

The issue is not whether we should continue to do what is working — it's whether we are prepared for what happens when things change. What do you need to know in order to be prepared, and where will that knowledge come from? And even more importantly, what else could we achieve if we continued to push further? What would we accomplish if we were not satisfied with our current levels of success — and instead set our goals much higher? We should all know by now that things will change. The world is constantly changing. And as the world changes, what we know and what we have been doing won't matter nearly as much. But we also know that we can also imagine a very different future and commit ourselves to working toward that new reality.

There is no perfect way to predict change or to anticipate what form the inevitable shifts will take. Some changes happen gradually, over generations. Other changes are sparked by events — catastrophic or otherwise — and the change manifests much more quickly. It is equally difficult to anticipate what knowledge you will need at the ready in order to adapt appropriately. One common mistake organizations make is to assign the task of thinking about the future to a special task force or a specific department. Just as everyone has imagination, everyone must share the responsibility for dreaming up new ways of doing business (or anything else for that matter).

You'll Know It When You See (or Hear, or Read, or Whatever) It

In his commencement address to Stanford University in June 2007, Dana Gioia, then head of the National Endowment for the Arts, spoke about "the fact that we live in a culture that barely acknowledges and rarely celebrates the arts or artists." He told the graduates:

> There is an experiment I'd love to conduct. I'd like to survey a cross-section of Americans and ask them how many active NBA players, Major League Baseball players, and *American Idol* finalists they can name.
>
> Then I'd ask them how many living American poets, playwrights, painters, sculptors, architects, classical musicians, conductors, and composers they can name.
>
> I'd even like to ask how many living American scientists or social thinkers they can name.
>
> Fifty years ago, I suspect that along with Mickey Mantle, Willie Mays, and Sandy Koufax, most Americans could have named, at the very least, Robert Frost, Carl Sandburg, Arthur Miller, Thornton Wilder, Georgia O'Keeffe, Leonard Bernstein, Leontyne Price, and Frank Lloyd Wright. Not to mention scientists and thinkers like Linus Pauling, Jonas Salk, Rachel Carson, Margaret Mead, and especially Dr. Alfred Kinsey.
>
> I don't think that Americans were smarter then, but American culture was. Even the mass media placed a

greater emphasis on presenting a broad range of human achievement.

Gioia went on to describe how he was exposed to comedians, popular singers, and movie stars, as well as classical musicians, opera singers, authors, and jazz greats — all while watching *The Ed Sullivan Show* and other variety shows on television. "All of these people were famous to the average American," he explained, "because the culture considered them important." That is no longer the case. He continued:

> Today no working-class or immigrant kid would encounter that range of arts and ideas in the popular culture. Almost everything in our national culture, even the news, has been reduced to entertainment, or altogether eliminated.
>
> The loss of recognition for artists, thinkers, and scientists has impoverished our culture in innumerable ways, but let me mention one. When virtually all of a culture's celebrated figures are in sports or entertainment, how few possible role models we offer the young.
>
> There are so many other ways to lead a successful and meaningful life that are not denominated by money or fame. Adult life begins in a child's imagination, and we've relinquished that imagination to the marketplace.[6]

Gioia warned that our nation was in a state of "cultural impoverishment" and that the economic and other damages that could result if we don't change course would be significant.

In 2014, China overtook the United States as the leading economic power in the world. Perhaps, China's growth was inevitable, considering the ebb and flow in the global economy or the fact that China's population is three times that of the United States or what Dana Gioia had warned about was happening. There are plenty of other indicators to suggest that the United States took its economic success for granted and became complacent. Three examples are given here:

- In the 1980s and 1990s, American companies and engineers were granted 10,000 more U.S. patents than foreign entities. In 2004, only four American companies ranked among the top 10 recipients of patents granted by the patent office. While the U.S. economy grew, and companies shifted their focus toward making money, businesses in other countries committed to creating new markets and opportunities that would pay off in the future.

- A total of 70% of engineers with PhDs who graduate from U.S. universities are foreign-born, and in countries like China, engineers hold many top political posts. In the United States, almost no engineers or scientists are engaged in high-level politics, and there is a virtual absence of engineers in our public policy debates. The United States, not anticipating the need to work better across sectors of society, faces challenges that other nations don't when it comes to capitalizing on new ideas.

- Furthermore, when it comes to its citizens' health the United States ranks below many other wealthy countries (33rd out of 145 countries with populations over 1 million people) and, as of the last U.S. Census report, 14.5% of Americans are impoverished — 45.3 million people. Even as the economy has grown and new advancements have been made, only some in the United States have benefited.

Gioia also suggested a way to prevent the decline that he predicted, telling the graduates "If the United States is to compete effectively with the rest of the world in the new global marketplace, it is not going to succeed through cheap labor or cheap raw materials, nor even the free flow of capital or a streamlined industrial base. To compete successfully, this country needs continued creativity, ingenuity, and innovation." The challenge that Gioia put to the graduates that day, and the lesson that we can all still take away from his speech, is that taking risks, and embracing culture, is part of our history, and that by using our imagination we can help to generate opportunities that will benefit everyone in the nation, and beyond.

Slow and Steady

The precursor to creativity, ingenuity, and innovation is imagination. We need to close The Imagination Gap — to unleash other amazing forces that will benefit our society, culturally and economically. We need to keep learning and preparing for whatever challenges we might face. That doesn't happen overnight — it happens over time, and it doesn't happen on its own. It requires leadership and patience.

There aren't many industries that have the benefit of patience as part of their operating mandate. One that does: museums, and in particular, large museums like the Metropolitan Museum of Art (the Met). As Sree Sreenivasan, the former Chief Digital Officer for the Met explained, "one thing that's different between the museum world and the corporate sector is the ability to be patient. When you live in a Profit-and-loss (P&L) world it's very different from being here. We do our best not to lose money but even more than that, there's a sense of purpose that we're doing something a lot longer." That sense of purpose comes from the top. The leadership of the museum believes that presenting the history of civilization is more important than squeezing every possible dollar out of a visitor. Along the same lines, Sreenivasan told me that the museum curators think of themselves as conservators. "They're preserving a vase not for a quarter, or a year — not even for decades. Their goal is like to keep this here for centuries." In other words, the Met is playing the longest game of all.

The benefit of having that kind of patience as a part of your way of doing things, Sreenivasan acknowledged, is that you have a "runway here that allows you to try things and to prove things out in ways that would be impossible in the business world. Nothing about museum life is exclusively transactional."

The downside is that not everyone, at times even the same people at the highest levels of the institution, appreciate the value of that patience.

There is no system that will work for everyone — especially when it comes to using your imagination. A step-by-step guide won't unlock what is hiding in the darkest and most interesting parts of your brain, and any time you set rules for how people should think, you are imposing limits on what you get back. It is the responsibility of the leadership of an organization, no matter the size or focus, to encourage people use and apply their imagination. The imagination gap is not the result of a systems failure. It is a leadership challenge.

The Met, like every other institution, must compete for customers (or visitors), employees, and attention. "One of the hardest things is to recruit, retain, inspire digital staff," explained Sreenivasan. The Met doesn't pay out bonuses and doesn't offer employees' equity, but it still must compete — especially in New York City — with Wall Street firms, big brands, and agencies, and, of course, tech companies like Google and Facebook. "What I have to do is explain how what we're doing here is so fantastic and so great — because of this really long, long runway that we have." Sreenivasan must find ways to demonstrate the important role that the Met plays in our society into something a potential recruit might value.

The challenge that the Met faces is no different than any other organization. Every organization needs to make the case that it adds value to the world, and that people who work there play an important role in driving those desired outcomes. That core argument begins at the top, and must be made by the leaders of an organization. Leaders must inspire people and help to create a culture that puts everyone in a position to be successful, and contribute beyond what their job description specifically outlines as their responsibilities. It is the leader's job to encourage people to use and apply their imagination, not for their own benefit, but in the interest of the organization as a whole.

Leaders are expected to be honest, confident, decisive, and inspiring. They should have the skills to communicate well, the wherewithal to delegate responsibility, and the confidence to be open and transparent. They should also use their imagination and apply it to their work — and do so in ways that inspire their employees, supporters, and followers to do the same.

Bill Gates, in a note to employees on the 40th anniversary of the founding Microsoft said that imagination played a big role in the success of the computer giant. He wrote: "Early on, Paul Allen and I set the goal of a computer on every desk and in every home. It was a bold idea and a lot of people thought we were out of our minds to imagine it was possible. It is amazing to think about how far computing has come since then, and we can all be proud of the role Microsoft played in that revolution." He then added that "To create a new standard, it takes something that's not just a little bit different; it takes something that's really new and really captures people's imagination."[7] That idea that came from his imagination, and became his passion, not only inspired Bill Gates, but also others at Microsoft, and other companies — resulting in the computing revolution.

Jim Koch, the founder of Sam Adams, told *Fast Company*, "Imagination is crucial to leadership because leadership requires energy and motivation and it requires giving people something exciting." He explained "For me, I imagined bringing great beer to the United States and I imagine a company that I would want to work for. And that was motivating to people. People were excited about the idea of making great beer in the United States and doing it in a company where they enjoyed coming to work every day, if only for the free beer."[8] When it comes to imagination, leadership means taking an idea and making it into something special — seeing the possibilities so clearly that you are able to overcome a barrage of skepticism and doubt.

The Broadway hit musical *Hamilton* is often cited as one of the most imaginative productions in the history of theater. What makes it so extraordinary? Two things.

First: the story. Alexander Hamilton came to this country as an immigrant, with a government that did not exist, fought in the revolution, and then created the American economic system.

Everyone told Hamilton he was crazy. But he didn't listen — he started to write out his ideas. Everyone said his system would destroy the young nation. But he didn't listen — he fought for his plan, debating anyone who challenged his views. That economic system is still to this day what drives the United States. He was the only one who had this concept in his head, and he made it possible for that idea to become a reality.

Second: the production. *Hamilton* is a groundbreaking work of imagination. The show is a biographical rendering of the life of founding father and U.S. treasury secretary set primarily to rap and hip-hop music. Lin-Manuel Miranda, the writer, composer, and star of *Hamilton*, told *The Atlantic* it "is a story about America then, told by America now."[9] The idea initially formed when Miranda read the biography of Alexander Hamilton, and imagined a hip-hop based musical presentation of the story.

When he first conceived of it, Lin-Manuel Miranda was told the idea would never work. Even Ron Chernow, the author of the biography, thought Miranda was crazy. But he didn't listen — he started writing out his ideas. Miranda imagined a cast comprised of African-American and Hispanic actors — which didn't reflect the reality of the historical figures, nor fit what you typically do in most Broadway musicals. Everyone told him it wasn't possible. He didn't listen — he started casting. From the moment it opened, *Hamilton* was celebrated for its vision. In just its first year, *Hamilton* became one of the most celebrated, critically acclaimed, and culturally influential Broadway musicals of our time, captured 11 Tony Awards — and its lasting legacy is still barely known.

Hamilton wouldn't have happened without Alexander Hamilton — whose imagination was needed to help create the critical structures that still help govern the United States. *Hamilton* wouldn't have happened without Lin-Manuel Miranda — whose imagination was needed to shape a production that is unlike anything ever presented. Both were leaders in their time, and have inspired others — not just in politics or the arts — to use their imagination and explore opportunities they had not considered before.

Drawing on the Right Minds

Giving people permission to use and apply their imagination is a critical step to unlocking potential and preparing for the future. That is true in every type of organization, no matter the size or focus. And it must be equally applied to every employee (or member, or student, or whatever) within an organization. Everyone must be encouraged and enabled to use and apply their imagination and contribute their ideas.

In 2011, Susan Wojcicki, at the time Google's Senior Vice President of Advertising (she is now the President of Google-owned YouTube), wrote about how the culture at Google encourages and enables employees to ask questions and explore new ideas, as well as aggressively pursue them in the most intelligent and organized way. She called the approach "Spark with Imagination, Fuel with Data." "In our fast-evolving market, it's hard for people to know, or even imagine, what they want. That's why we recruit people who believe the impossible can become a reality," Wojcicki wrote.

Using an example of one of the Google engineers who first proposed the idea of driverless vehicles (an idea that Google is now, five-plus years later, aggressively pursuing), Wojicki explained "We try to encourage this type of blue-sky thinking through '20 percent time' — a full day a week during which engineers can work on whatever they want. Looking back at our launch calendar over a recent six-month period, we found that many products started life in employees' 20 percent time."[10]

Google's idea of devoting 20% of employees' time to nonrevenue generating ventures started with Larry Page and Sergey Brin. The company's founders wrote in Google's 2004 IPO letter: "We encourage our employees, in addition to their regular projects, to spend 20% of their time working on what they think will most benefit Google. This empowers them to be more creative and innovative. Many of our significant advances have happened in this manner." Google News and Gmail are the most well-known products that emerged from 20% time, but the long list of concepts that never developed into anything marketable, but did inspire and inform other concepts and improvements throughout the Google universe (and beyond), is arguably even more valuable.

Innovation experts and advocates have held up Google's 20% commitment as something any organization can do to generate a constant feed of new ideas, and improve company culture (making it easier to recruit and retain the best talent). The idea of 20% time at Google is not even strictly managed nor are employees mandated to spend time dreaming up or exploring things outside their day-to-day responsibilities. The 20% time is neither scheduled nor measured as part of Google's employee reviews. "In some ways, the idea of 20 percent time is more important than the reality of it," wrote Google's head of People Operations (aka HR), Laszlo Bock, in his book, *Work Rules!* "It operates somewhat outside the lines of formal management oversight, and always will, because the most talented and creative people can't be forced to work."[11] What Google understands, and everyone else should begin to recognize, is that when employees use and apply their imagination, they not only produce new ideas for potential products, but also become more invested in the success of the company and their role in that work.

In an article for *Harvard Business Review* entitled "Creativity and the Role of the Leader,"[12] Teresa Amabile and Mukti Khaire, professor and assistant professor, respectively, at Harvard Business School, wrote that a big reason that companies don't embrace imagination and its byproducts (including creativity) more is because it has been "considered unmanageable—too elusive and intangible to pin down—or because concentrating on it produced a less immediate payoff than improving execution, it hasn't been the focus of most managers' attention."

They added, "by definition the ability to create something novel and appropriate… is essential to the entrepreneurship that gets new businesses started and that sustains the best companies after they have reached global scale." If you want to break through, disrupt, or transform any part of our society, or keep a company competitive in a rapidly and constantly changing world, a key component of your strategy will need to encourage people to use and apply their imaginations.

The secret, according to Amabile and Khaire, is that companies like Google encourage all of its employees to think and act like entrepreneurs. From the top down, imagination is a key attribute that fuels the success of the company. They cite a study by Google's founders that tracked the progress of ideas that they had backed versus ideas that had been executed without formal support from management. The results showed a higher success rate from ideas that began with, and stayed with, employees.[13]

Importantly though, Google is not trying to dictate how their employees use or apply imagination. They give employees permission, and encouragement, to explore their interests but don't over-structure or impose strict parameters. They also make clear that the types of projects that Google wants most, and that employees should be spending their time on, are the ones that will produce the most novel outcomes. The idea of structuring how people use their imagination is what kills it — and it's the mistake that organizations make when trying to force innovation into their organization. The rules, forced collaboration, and other tricks of the trade that have come to define the professional innovation industry have the opposite effect. There is no user manual for what might happen.

Knowledge and Systems

It is tempting to suggest that employees must be allowed to roam freely, and that metrics should be removed from any conversation so as to preserve our ability to use and apply our imagination to the fullest. But in reality, an organization will benefit from having some structure to help manage how they empower employees (or members, or supporters) to use and apply their imagination. The same is true for leaders who want to encourage new ideas without tying them to short-term measurable outcomes; there must be some roadmap that they can follow.

There aren't seven steps that every person can follow or a cookie-cutter design for a workspace that an organization can build out to optimize knowledge intake. There can be a systematic approach to building knowledge — but the systems must change and adapt constantly. Rita King, the head of Science House, a strategic consultancy that calls itself a "cathedral of imagination," says the key is to introduce "unknown, uncertainty, unfamiliarity, mystery — the emotions that cause fear or exhilaration." King designs activities for clients that "allow for serendipity to chance, events unfold in a happier beneficial way." When someone is experiencing the types of emotions associated with uncertainty, unfamiliarity, and mystery, they are outside their comfort zone, which means new knowledge will follow.

Not every client that King works with is ready to dive in to using their own imagination. In those cases, King says, you have to show them what it means to try something new. She described a project where a client (in the hotel industry) asked for help to generate new ideas for their business — but made clear they didn't want to be involved in the process themselves because they weren't very good at coming up with new, creative ideas. King didn't argue with her client or enroll them in a training program. Instead, King and her colleagues decided the best option was to use their own imaginations — and provide their client with a report on their experience.

The team ventured out on road trip and instituted only one rule: say yes to anything they were asked to do. "We ended up going to a community theater in Mississippi. We went to people's houses for dinner. It was insane the number of things we did. And then when we talked to our client about what it was like to say yes for 11 days, they started to come up with new ideas as well."

Very often, the process of using and applying imagination is mystifying to people. People are told they don't have a good imagination, or the other people are better suited to use their knowledge to feed creative thinking. It is not true. "When you explain to someone that self-sabotage is part of what keeps people from exploring, their perspective changes," says King, "They want to know more because in that moment, they begin to understand they are actually the problem." By sharing her experiences from that trip, King helped her client gain new knowledge and perspective — even without directly participating. By seeing how others were using their imagination, King's client recognized they had plenty of new things to learn, and that the outputs of imagination were tangible. With that new knowledge, their imagination started to fire as well.

Learn the Skills, Unlock the Potential

In any professional role, there are skills that an employee must have in order to complete the work. Most of the time, those skills are only a small fraction of what it takes to get the job done. The balance is made up by how the individual employee understands and attacks the task at hand. Skills can be taught.

A lot of different skills are required to create a movie. Those skills, once learned, open up the possibility of creating anything one can imagine. As Johanna Schwartz, an award-winning documentary filmmaker, explained:

> You can learn the technical skills for filmmaking. You can learn the ways that you can produce a film, like raising money, getting people on board, getting people excited, how to work the equipment, of course, and all that. You can almost even teach empathy just by giving people knowledge that they didn't have before. But I think being a great filmmaker is about more than just having empathy, more than just caring about the subject matter — and certainly more than just capturing and editing a story. I think you need to be able to see — you need to be able to understand if someone is going to be a good vehicle for the stories, that this person is going to be a good character.

Schwartz describes each film as its own journey. A project might start with a chance encounter or a nugget of an idea from the filmmaker — but what follows is an arduous process filled with planning, scripting, production, and more. It's not just the knowledge or skills. "I don't know if it can be taught," Schwartz told me. "At the end of it, they may or may not get there," referring to how filmmakers are full of ideas, many of which never translate into films. "What is the difference between having an idea and turning it into a film? A lot of time it's the filmmakers imagination."

The capacity to use your imagination in the professional context, as an engineer working at Google or a filmmaker trying to translate a story onto the screen, is the same that a child uses when trying to make sense of the world. "As a child, you don't know what you don't know. So, if you're never exposed to something, if you don't believe it's a reality, then you may not ever believe that it can be your reality," Bradley Feinstein, an entrepreneur, told me when explaining the unlimited potential that children have to use their imagination to learn about and explore the world. But as they grow older, and more structure is imposed to dictate what someone must know, or the knowledge they must possess in order to succeed, that sense of wonder begins to disappear.

"I think we have this tendency to take these highly creative careers and then, maybe it's ease, maybe it's convenience, maybe it's a change in priorities, but we pull the creativity out of them and it just becomes this kind of autopilot mentality," Feinstein offered. "Let's say I have this beautifully imaginative idea and I need money to go make it a reality. Most likely the people that are giving me the money believe in the idea, and me. But, there are going to be metrics, a growth model, margins, returns and other things that have to be determined before any money is committed. The imagination is removed — and replaced with numbers. When that happens, that beautifully imaginative idea becomes like everything else, a business."

When you consider who are the people that our society holds up as being the most imaginative, the ones that have incredible vision, they will almost always fall outside of the formal structure. They won't necessarily be the ones most people can cite as the leading experts on an issue. They won't necessarily work in the arts or hold the title of creative director at an ad agency or PR firm either. They may not even — by traditional measures — be considered successful because of their ideas. We are more likely to recognize and celebrate the best examples of what we are already comfortable with — the displays of creativity, innovation, and more — than we are to embrace the people who are truly imaginative and the work they are doing to challenge what we know and expect today.

Sometimes Less Really Is More

In a factory setting, predictability and accountability are highly valued. The job assigned is to do the same thing over and over again. The more efficient the approach is, the better the outcome. Factories make money by perfecting the repetition. In any other organization, the value of repetition diminishes over time. Perhaps it's a holdover from the industrial era, but the first instinct most organizations have when they consider how to grow or maximize their success is to institute more process. The standardization and continuous improvement of "the way things are done" occupies at least some part of every organization today. But for all the perceived benefits of achieving greater efficiency, repetition also creates an environment where there is little willingness to try something new.

In a study of U.S. and European companies, The Boston Consulting Group found that "over the past fifteen years, the amount of procedures, vertical layers, interface structures, coordination bodies, and decision approvals needed ... has increased by anywhere from 50 percent to 350 percent." What's more, in the most complicated organizations, "managers spend 40 percent of their time writing reports and 30 percent to 60 percent of it in coordination meetings."[14] There is such a premium placed on being able to measure and continually optimize performance, that management has become an industry on its own, and not just a function that helps to keep an organization running smoothly.

For their *Harvard Business Review* articles about creativity and leadership, Teresa Amabile and Mukti Khaire talked to Mark Fishman, MD, President of the Novartis Institutes for BioMedical Research about this subject. He was unsparing in his criticism of such structured systems, calling one high-profile system in particular to task. "If there is one device that has destroyed more innovation than any other, it is Six Sigma" Fishman offered, referring to the infamous business management concept created in 1986 by an engineer at Motorola, and later embraced by companies across numerous industries (most notably Jack Welch who introduced Six Sigma as CEO of General Electric in 1995).

The central idea behind Six Sigma is that if you can measure how many defects you have in a process, you can systematically figure out how to eliminate them and get as close to zero defects as possible. Fishman says that "Efficient models make good sense for the middle and end stages of the innovation process, when the game has moved from discovery to control and reliability" — but should not be used at the beginning of any process, when imagination and the opening up of new possibilities is most important.

Moreover, when organizations focus on process improvements too much, or too early, it has a chilling effect on everything else. When people try to avoid duplication of effort, they eliminate any variability in how to approach a challenge. But as circumstances change, or when the challenge facing an organization requires more than just greater efficiency to address, the variability ultimately has the most value. "The poster child here is Kodak, which kept making the process of manufacturing and distributing chemical-based film more efficient instead of devoting attention to making the shift to digital photography," Fishman said. "In other words, it kept getting better and better at doing the wrong thing."

Everyone recognizes that different processes, skill sets, and even technology must be embraced throughout an organization in order to remain competitive, adapt as times change, and encourage collaboration. What does that look like in practice? How do you allow people to pursue their passions, while also getting their work done? How can you provide an appreciative and engaged audience for new ideas, while also staying focused on your goals?

Simple: you just make it happen. Every opportunity should be considered. Every person who uses and applies their imagination should be celebrated. Ideas must be pursued, and even if they fail to pan out, the lessons from the experience must be considered and shared.

Michael Gump argues that for people to be most comfortable using and applying their imagination, they need to "feel self-confident, and to know that they can do things. That's really positive, and it helps to move them forward." Gump also argues that everyone's job is to bring your best ideas, but not to be married to them. "You have to be open to feedback. And, in the end, it might not be what you thought you were doing when you set out, but it doesn't make it wrong."

Imagination and Your Daily Routine

Using and applying our imagination is important in both our work and nonwork life. We are also equally likely to over-organize our personal lives, when we aren't on the clock or have a manager or higher-up to blame. There may not be a Six Sigma to assess our personal time use and decision-making, but we still fall into patterns.

Your morning routine is a perfect example. Day after day you do the same thing: wake up, check your phone, flip on the morning news, hop in the shower, get dressed, pack your bag, grab the newspaper, and head out the door. You might make little adjustments, but the pattern at large goes unchanged. There are benefits for sure. A strict routine prevents a buildup of stress — you can rely on your muscle memory to take of what's needed, without letting anything else get in the way. That's why Mark Zuckerberg famously wears the same gray t-shirt every day. And similarly, President Obama told Vanity Fair "You'll see I wear only gray or blue suits. I'm trying to pare down decisions. I don't want to make decisions about what I'm eating or wearing. Because I have too many other decisions to make."[15] The existence of a routine makes it possible for people — including Mark Zuckberg and

President Obama, though it would be just as applicable to anyone else — to use and apply their imagination to other, arguably, more important matters.

For similar reasons, people tend to keep their morning routine simple and structured. A simple morning routine allows maximum time to wake up and prepare for the day ahead. But, what if our morning routine actually blocks our imagination from getting engaged? According to a study published in the journal *Thinking and Reasoning* in 2012, that's exactly what happens. In the journal article, researchers Mareike Wieth and Rose Zacks reported that imaginative insights are most likely to come to us when we're groggy and unfocused.[16] They explain that the mental processes that inhibit distracting or irrelevant thoughts are at their weakest in these moments, allowing unexpected and sometimes inspired connections to be made. The research describes sleepy people having "more diffuse attentional focus" that allows them to "widen their search through their knowledge network. This widening leads to an increase in creative problem solving." Put another way, the sharper you and your thinking are, the less likely your imagination is to go wild.

A loud, stressful, chaotic commute — whether you are sitting in traffic surrounded by honking cars or stuffed onto a bus with sharp-elbowed fellow passengers — doesn't help either. When your stress level rises, the amount of cortisol in your brain goes up — damaging your brain cells, slowing down the speed with which signals are transmitted between neurons. That means your ability to mashup different pieces of knowledge in your brain slows down resulting in the formation of fewer imaginative ideas.

The takeaway is this: the best routine is one of complete and utter spontaneity. No routine at all. Or as Jeff DeGraff, a researcher from the University of Michigan offered, "It's not that there isn't a process; it's that there are millions of micro-processes. It's like a play book. There are a lot of different ways people have organized their cognitive processes and a lot of different experiences." The more you switch your patterns, the more likely you are to trigger the parts of your brain that will generate new, compelling ideas.

> ## Challenge: Look Deep. Look Twice
>
> It is pretty common for people to tell you NOT to get stuck on one thing. They caution against staying in one place in the hopes that something might occur. But, sometimes you need to jump down the rabbit hole and get lost in a subject. When you commit to focusing on one thing at a time, you are prompted to think in new ways. You observe things differently.
>
> *To Do*: Force yourself to stay in one place for an extended period of time. Watch every episode of every season of a new show on demand. Don't worry about what else you might need to do that day, just be in the moment and see what happens.

NOTES

1. http://opinionator.blogs.nytimes.com/2010/08/15/reclaiming-the-imagination/?_r=0
2. https://www.brainpickings.org/2016/05/06/ursula-k-le-guin-freedom-oppression-storytelling/
3. The 9–11 Commission Report. http://govinfo.library.unt.edu/911/report/index.htm
4. Interview with Alec Ross — July 17, 2016.
5. http://archive.fortune.com/2006/07/05/magazines/fortune/imaginationeconomy.fortune/index.htm
6. http://news.stanford.edu/news/2007/june20/gradtrans-062007.html
7. http://www.theverge.com/2015/4/3/8340975/bill-gates-microsoft-40th-anniversary
8. http://www.fastcompany.com/3011466/30-second-mba/jim-koch-what-is-the-role-of-imagination-in-leadership
9. http://www.theatlantic.com/entertainment/archive/2015/09/lin-manuel-miranda-hamilton/408019/
10. *How Does Google Stay Innovative* — https://www.thinkwithgoogle.com/articles/8-pillars-of-innovation.html
11. http://www.businessinsider.com/google-20-percent-time-policy-2015-4
12. https://hbr.org/2008/10/creativity-and-the-role-of-the-leader

13. http://static.googleusercontent.com/media/research.google.com/en//pubs/archive/41469.pdf
14. http://www.fastcompany.com/1837301/5-ways-process-killing-your-productivity
15. http://www.vanityfair.com/news/2012/10/michael-lewis-profile-barack-obama
16. http://digest.bps.org.uk/2012/01/youre-most-creative-when-youre-at-your.html

Closing the Gap

We must close the Imagination Gap in order to open up the possibility of creating meaningful, measurable change — at all levels, in all sectors. This chapter introduces the strategic and operational requirements for closing the Imagination Gap, including: a different approach to the challenges that exist, better communication, engagement that applies imagination at every turn, a shift in the culture and behavior that we find acceptable and the standards against which to measure progress, and the development or redevelopment of structures and rules to govern and manage effectively in an uncertain future.

Each year, the South by Southwest Interactive Festival (SXSW) in Austin, Texas, attracts a unique mix of people from the world of technology, design, media, film, music, education, and an increasing number of people associated with the worlds of philanthropy and social change. SXSW offers a unique opportunity for different sectors to share ideas and partner on efforts related to addressing the most interesting and serious issues facing our global society. In other words, SXSW has the potential to be the ultimate playground for people trying to solve complex problems and have a meaningful, measurable impact on the world.

The most notable attendee in 2016 was President Barack Obama, who used his Keynote Conversation on the first day of the event to implore attendees to apply their expertise in ways that help expand the reach and impact of both government and the civic-minded organizations. The President went to SXSW to connect with the people who are shaping the digital environment, and who understand how best to influence behavior and drive actions. He called on them to work to figure out ways to get more people engaged in meaningful ways, explaining, "We cannot solve the problems in government and we cannot solve the problems that we face collectively as a society unless we, the people, are paying attention."

The President's message resonated — the best and brightest could be heard in the days that followed talking about how to answer the call and get involved. But what is required to solve these problems, and how to overcome the barriers standing in the way getting government, the private sector, and nonprofits, to better coordinate, is anything but clear.

Each sector has unique expertise and important perspective that, when combined, create an environment where durable solutions can be developed. But there are also obvious disconnects when it comes to how the expertise and resources from one sector might be combined with another. The potential for progress is at risk of being squandered. A big reason for our failure to maximize these opportunities is our lack of imagination when it comes to how to work together to address these critical issues.

The thousands of smart, passionate, talented people who descend on Austin each March are not committed to solving the most interesting and important problems. The reason has nothing to do with the complexity of the challenges — ending poverty or transforming democracy is more interesting and difficult to tackle than building an app to make it easier to order your dinner, or programming an algorithm to recommend the best outfit given the weather forecast. The reason is because even the best and brightest programmers, designers, filmmakers, and more struggle to find ways to use and apply their imagination in the world today.

SXSW is often credited with being an incubator, or an accelerator, for some of the most market-changing technologies. But the conversation about the role technology can play in serving humanity has not produced the same types of breakthrough ideas. The conversation at SXSW is focused on building awareness for causes, telling stories, and raising funds for short-term relief — traditional modes of delivering impact that have long dominated business and social sectors alike. Unfortunately, greater awareness of a cause does not, by itself, motivate people to take action. Money alone will not be enough to eradicate a disease. And when new technology platforms are introduced (the hot thing in 2016 has been virtual reality), focusing on how to use them to spread information instead of attacking the root of a problem, wastes precious time and energy. The list of things that need to change within any issue or cause is long, and getting longer. Meanwhile, we lack the bold, new, ambitious approaches that could shift the whole trajectory of these issues. We aren't doing anything that we have never been done before.

There are so many ways that SXSW could help change the way we think, operate, and organize around big ideas, exciting new tools, and important issues, thanks to its community of smart, passionate people. SXSW's original goal was "to create an event that would act as a tool for creative people and the companies they work with to develop their careers, to bring together people from a wide area to meet and share ideas." And in a lot of ways, they are doing that — disrupting our thinking around how technology can be used, creativity should be applied, what communications can achieve, and more. But we have barely scratched the surface of what is possible if we really think beyond our current way of doing things.

We must all work to close the Imagination Gap. Every organization, regardless of sector, is focused too much on small things — how many followers they have, whether they hit their quarterly sales goals, or how to gain greater efficiency or scale of their existing offerings. They are all failing to think bigger.

Closing the imagination gap requires (at least) three critical things: (1) acknowledging and understanding the gaps — and recognizing the difference between pursuing innovation and using your imagination; (2) sustained commitment to providing the proper care and feeding of our imagination; and (3) applying our imagination — not once, but actively and consistently in everything we do.

Innovation Is Not Imagination

In his book, *Understanding Media: The Extensions of Man*,[1] media and technology futurist Marshall McLuhan identified four attributes of innovation. He said innovation enhances something, eliminates something, returns us to something in our past, and/or over time reverses into its opposite. The best innovations embody all four attributes, and when applied effectively, a commitment to pursuing innovation inside an organization — whether it's a business, nonprofit, government agency, or school — can deliver new products and ways of achieving things that wouldn't happen, or happen as quickly, on their own.

Not surprisingly, when organizations start to show the benefits of innovation, others in their sector, and sometimes in other sectors as well, gain interest and started to embrace the approach as well. All it takes is another organization to gain an advantage to motivate others to want to catch back up. For the past decade, it seems every organization has created some sort of innovation team, embraced an innovation-related philosophy, or at least preached the value of innovation in their work. But the excitement around innovation is not entirely a good thing.

Bill Taylor, a cofounder of *Fast Company* magazine, wrote in 2012 "The dynamic is always the same ... A genuinely original strategy is born in one company or industry, consultants discover the practice and turn it into a marketable commodity, executives in all sorts of other companies race to 'buy' the product — and then they wonder why the technique didn't work nearly as well in their organization as it did in the place that created it in the first place."[2] He cautioned that "the moment that 'innovation' becomes just another leadership program, yet another consultant-driven management technique, one more piece of language in ... the 'jargon monoxide' that defines so much of business life, it ceases to be a positive force for change."

Bill Taylor's fears have been realized. The very idea of innovation has become commoditized. Pursuing any sort of change, incremental as it may be, is celebrated as progress. But the actual impact of whatever that innovation is producing is minimal at best.

"This idea of innovation is overused. Everybody says they're an innovator. But it's not true." Sree Sreenivasan told me. Sreenivasan has twice been tapped to help pull old, storied institutions – Columbia University and the Metropolitan Museum of Art — into the modern age. He also happens to be married to an innovation consultant. Still, he doesn't buy into the hype that has formed around the idea of innovation in seemingly every sector. "Everybody thinks that ... you can just throw innovation at it and fix it and that's not the case." Some approach to innovation can be applied, by anyone, at any time, in a variety of different ways, but that does not guarantee that it will have any meaningful impact.

Sreenivasan and I spoke while he was still the Chief Digital Officer for the Metropolitan Museum of Art — the first ever to hold the position (he has since left his role at the Met). He explained that his team was charged with changing how the Met approached their work — and that his hope was that some of what they tried would also filter out to other museums and cultural institutions. He also stressed that that none of what they were doing was new, but in terms of the world of museums, even some of the simple things were considered groundbreaking. "One of the leaps that has been made here by our director is to say that the value of every visitor in person or online is exactly the same. That is stunning because it's not, they don't cost the same. A visitor coming in gives you money. A visitor visiting online costs you money. Right there is a pretty big leap for the museum world, to say that the digital is as important as the physical. That has never been articulated in any place that I know where you are trying to sell tickets to a space."

In other words, something may be innovative, but that does not make it imaginative.

Joseph Schumpeter, one of the most influential economists of the 20th century believed that innovation was about the commercialization of an idea, or as Noah Brier, an entrepreneur and the founder of Percolate, explained it, "It was about finding a market for an invention. In his world innovation was part of this three-step process where you have inventors, you have innovators, and you have diffusors. Inventors create things. Innovators find markets for inventions. And diffusors bring new inventions to market."

Schumpeter described innovation as a form of "creative destruction" that serves to restructure a whole market system and favors those who grasp the changes the fastest. He wrote: "the problem that is usually visualized is how capitalism administers existing structures, whereas the relevant problem is how it creates and destroy them."[3]

Brier made clear that much of what is considered "new" today is really just incremental change or improvements on what already exists. "In pure terms, most of what you do is combine existing elements. You are very seldom inventing from scratch. You are working off an existing structure. You are working off a set of tools. You are working off an open source code library, and an open source programming language, and maybe an open source framework and whatever else. You are using all of these tools," he explained. But his interest is in making of something new, creating things that have never been done before. And for that, you have to think beyond markets and disruption and tap into your imagination.

The Gap Is Real, and it's Spectacular

David Slocum, the Faculty Director of Executive MBA Program at the Berlin School of Creative Leadership, wrote back in 2014 that we were running into an innovation problem.

> Innovation is everywhere, from mission and vision statements to strategic positioning and brand marketing to team charters and individual performance goals. Likewise, creativity, often in adjectival form, has become a necessary qualifier for nearly all aspects of management and operations: leadership, strategy, talent management, organizational design, customer or client relationships, collaboration, and teamwork. Even creative accounting has become a worthy aspiration (just not "too" creative …).

Slocum warned that the cult-like thinking around innovation and creativity would continue to grow, while what it produces would not keep up. "One consequence is what Bill O'Connor, of Autodesk, calls 'innovation pornography,' in which too many people become voyeurs, rapturously watching others innovate without doing so themselves," Slocum writes. "Another is the myth that creativity and original thinking can solve any problem or develop an idea the world will eventually embrace."

Slocum was right, but he also knew that accepting innovation was not going to be enough to truly change how organizations are operating. So, in addition to his argument, he called on business and other leaders to acknowledge what was happening — and what it really meant to their future. He challenged leaders to ask themselves a series of questions, about what they plan to accomplish, how to measure their impact, and even what language they use to position and describe their efforts.

> Thoughtful leaders have long recognized the value of auditing their current innovation or creativity activities, needs and capabilities. As time has passed and both words have been used more and more, it is also useful to conduct such an innovation and creativity *language* audit. What do you mean when you say that innovation is a core value or a strategic priority? What does specifying creative talent development mean for the shape and orientation of a HR processes or organizational learning? More generally, how does innovation or creativity practically differentiate decisions, behaviors and results?

Better understanding and clarity is needed around the concept of innovation, when and how it is used — and when it is not the right approach for what needs to be achieved. It is critical that we distinguish the skills that contribute to creativity or pursuing innovative solutions and the larger, embedded ability we all have to use and apply our imagination. When we do that, we stop trying to structure the approach to imagination or force it into every conversation, and instead open up the possibility of more seriously considering the important role that imagination plays in transforming our world.

Slocum's questions show the important differences between innovation and imagination. Innovation and imagination are complementary for sure, and can contribute to each other. Still, innovation is about pursuing the incremental, continuous, improvements — to a process, a product, or really anything. Imagination is about creating something novel and seemingly more ambitious — an idea, a concept, or an image of the future. Ideas born from the imagination must ultimately be pursued to become real, and that requires creativity and innovative thinking. But the constant optimization and improvement that drives innovation is built on top of something that is already in place. It is a reapplication of something that exists. Imagination is about introducing or achieving something that has never been done or even considered.

A big reason for the imagination gap is the lack of clarity that Slocum describes. A critical first step is to recognize and acknowledge the distinction.

Applying Imagination

There is a relationship between the linear, structured approach to getting things done and the act of considering and exploring new ideas. The likely problems you face when it comes to execution is finding out you don't have the proper skills, tools, or resources to get the job done. The greatest challenge when it comes to imagination isn't that people lack the ability or capacity, but that we seem to be afraid to even try. There are a lot of people who have ideas — there are even idea-holics who can't stop generating new questions and options to consider — but when those ideas are not considered useful, practical, or pursuable to a specific issue, people are afraid to even suggest them.

Almost anyone you ask will say they are absolutely open to hearing new ideas. But when pressed, the willingness to seriously consider or invest any energy in pursuing new ideas is more limited. Before launching into any effort, most people want to know for sure that it will be worth the risk. They want hypothetical certainty that they will be successful. Achieving hypothetical certainty might involve creating renderings or models of what you plan to build, populating spreadsheets with seemingly reasonable numbers and projections, mapping out the anticipated steps that would follow as an idea is explored further — and the results of the actions that you would propose to take. Of course, it's all made up. You don't know what will happen in the future, or how a step you take will unfold or what the response would be. The quest to achieve hypothetical certainty is just your imagination at work.

When you generate a new idea, do you really have any concept of how to bring it to fruition? How do you get from an idea to having something real, and in the process confirm that what you are doing is still novel? These sound like innocuous questions but they're what Jeff DeGraff calls rabbit-hole questions — meaning that they can easily take you, or your organization, off task and deep into thinking about a situation and what value the business is trying to produce. People are capable of having those hypothetical conversations; we all have an imagination to draw on for inspiration. But the certainty part and the skills and expertise to build, edit, draw, project, calculate, model, and whatever else is needed to predict the future to the satisfaction of others are not something everyone possesses.

What ends up happening, more often than not, is that our most imaginative ideas slowly get converted into practical innovations. The diminishing of those ideas isn't done intentionally, perhaps not even consciously, but it happens because of how we go about trying to achieve hypothetical certainty.

"How you apply your imagination is going to be very different if you are a designer than if you are an engineer. I think part of the problem is that we label people, and that influences their thinking," says Noah Brier. "If you were to ask someone who is more creative, a designer or an engineer? They would say a designer because when we talk about creativity, we generally talk about the visual arts more than we would talk about creativity in code." We also label people when it comes to imagination, often describing them crazy or even reckless because their ideas are not closely tied to our current understanding or experience. A critical step toward closing the imagination gap will include changing the labels we use, and how we classify new ideas.

"I think there's an issue of courage," Jeff DeGraff offered. "There's an issue of risk that's involved when you start having ideas that are probably not socially acceptable" — which is how almost all ideas that have not been heard or pursued before get categorized. But ideas are just that, thoughts that have emerged and been suggested. Applying your imagination, and having the courage to explore new territory, is not easy. Lots of people have novel ideas, but few have the courage to pursue them.

Seeing Around the Corner

In real time, bold, imaginative ideas are seen as crazy. With the benefit of history the ideas, and the people who generate them, get reclassified as genius. Or as Rita J. King told me, "Every great solution works. That's what makes it great."

Part of people's unwillingness to embrace imagination is a practical one — because the idea has not taken shape yet as something real, it can't easily be seen, held, or experimented with. In the 1960s, when President Kennedy challenged the Americans to send a man to the moon, the idea was considered crazy — but people understood it because the moon, and even the idea of space exploration, was already understood. While reaching the moon had never been achieved, everyone could look up in the sky each night and see the goal before them.

New ideas are more fully appreciated and embraced when they are grounded in our current experience. "That's why we measure the number of people who are using Uber instead of talking about the transformative effect that ride-sharing is having on cities as a whole," Rita J. King suggested. "We understand the idea of people taking a car from one place to the other. We are good at measuring the intrinsic characteristics of something, but not the extrinsic consequences of something. You need imagination to understand the impact." She noted that in 20 years there will likely be many fewer parking spots because of services like Uber, and technological advancements like driverless cars. Still, people can't imagine a totally redesigned cityscape, so that discussion rarely gets raised.

The increasingly integrated role that technology is playing in our lives along with the availability of data is contributing a new way of seeing the world. We are all connected, which also means we can measure and compare and consider everything at an extraordinarily detailed level. That is driving a sense of inevitability that technology will only further become enmeshed in how we live and think. Still, much of the way we function as a society today, and the way our institutions are structured, is quite an analog still. Our behaviors are overwhelming influenced by past actions, not oriented around the future and what could possibly occur. We spent most of our time responding, not predicting or preparing for what might happen next.

For example, right now we develop algorithms to influence our search results — which helps to find the best available restaurants or match our music choices to our workout routine. We can calculate how long it takes to drive from location A to B, and monitor traffic and other factors in real time to make the ride as enjoyable as possible. But those are all ways to apply technology and data to solve known problems or challenges. It doesn't take into account what we don't know might happen or what we could imagine as being possible. For example, before long, we won't be satisfied with just measuring how many cars there are on the road each day, because we will be able to look at each individual trip and understand the needs of commuters in a much more specific way. Similarly, treatment plans for diseases like cancer will be tailored to individuals, dramatically improving the efficacy of those efforts.

What else might algorithms be able to tell us about who we are as people? When are we going to create tools and systems that get ahead of educational and health-care problems? When you have billions of people that need to be fed or resettled, you need more than just a novel idea, you need an imagination that can scale.

That is something our society has never done well — and there is little evidence that further innovation and optimization will dramatically change the trajectory that we are on, generally or with regard to any specific issue. The best option is to figure out how to integrate with technology to create something new. What do we want to know about ourselves? The key is to imagine what we don't know yet.

The goal must be to see around the corner.

What do people with active imaginations do differently than others? How do we get people to go after truly monumental endeavors? How do we change what they aspire to? Kurt Ronn, a creative entrepreneur and committed philanthropist, says we just have to make the commitment to doing more with an eye toward the future. "A lot of people think there are rules in place that are stopping them from using their imagination. That's not true – it's in their head," he told me. "If I gave you a box of crayons and a piece of paper, and I had the same box of crayons and piece of paper here, we could both draw a picture and then compare it. We could show it to each other and see that we both had some idea of what to create. Unfortunately, because of how the world currently works, someone will come along and decide that one of us is a better artist than the other one. We have to stop doing that."

Instead of comparing ideas, or judging one to be better than the other — based on our current understanding of the world — we should be able to consider each individual's capacity to use and apply their imagination. We should be able to understand what each person aspires to be, and shape our social behaviors so that everyone feels empowered to think big.

Culture of Imagination

We have a culture today that does not appreciate, value, or really know what to do with imagination. "There is a culture in American business, an approach that's committed to reckless pragmatism. Creativity and innovation have been designated to very specific roles," explains Dia Simms, the President of Combs Wine & Spirits, part of the business empire of Sean "Diddy" Combs, "and the mistake would be for the same thing to happen to imagination. No one is going to stand in a shareholder's meeting and speak at length about something that feels like hocus pocus and can't be very easily measured. I don't think it is a matter of an inside or an outside thing. It is a way that we have historically approached being taken seriously in large businesses." That approach to business culture has become so ingrained, in every sector, that most people don't even consider the prospect of organizations operating in any other way.

Jamie Rose, an award-winning photographer and the co-founder of Momenta Group, believes "the saddest part about the creative industry today is the forceful relationship between clients and the teams that they work for." Rose argues that creative roles are now more about production than exploring new opportunities. "When people are hiring creatives, they say 'We want you to do it exactly this way' – and its almost always based on something they have seen before. Any talented professional in their field can do that." The alternative, according to Rose, is to present the challenge differently. "They should be asking 'What would you do?' They should be explaining their likes their dislikes and the parameters of the assignment. They should be asking the creative 'What would you recommend?' "

Marty Neumeier, the Director of Transformation at Liquid Agency and author of several books on brand, design, innovation, and creativity, has spent his career in leading brand and creative projects for clients of all types and sizes. He acknowledges, "We just don't have the habits, the culture and so forth that encourage our use of imagination." He offered the following diagnosis:

> Inventing new options in between knowing and doing is the key. And that's what's missing in most companies. They just move right into action as fast as possible and they don't want deal with the pain of developing something new because it's frustrating. It's depressing sometimes. It's hard work. But that's how it happens. It

happens because you focus on that place between knowing and doing.

Organizations are loathe to change, particularly when current (and historical) evidence seems to suggest that the path they are on is working. Even those who are open to change are not likely to volunteer to be first. That's why companies that are making money won't pursue new ideas on the prospect that they will need to offer different options to customers in the future — only to find themselves, and their industry, having been disrupted by an upstart competitor. Think of Blockbuster and Netflix, Kodak and the iPhone, and Snapchat and traditional media companies. There are numerous examples, and more that will emerge in the coming years for sure.

The best opportunity for shifting the culture around imagination will be showing the public's interest and willingness to embrace new ways of thinking — not waiting around for proof that an existing product or way of operating is no longer sustainable.

Be a Deviant

Jeff DeGraff, a University of Michigan Professor who studies innovation and behavior, explains that when we build systems to try and make us more innovative, we are actually making ourselves less innovative. "By definition systems eliminate variation. The systems are created not to make us more innovative; they are created to mitigate risk," he notes. That's why we cannot create systems that dictate specifically how we must use our imagination, or seek to apply imagination in specific or limited ways. For imagination to truly flourish, our use and application have to be mostly unbound.

As Rita J. King explains, "Imagination is the sand box that says, 'My goal is this over here. I have to get there somehow and I don't know how I'm going to get there, but I will consider doing whatever it takes to get there.' " Achieving that goal, in whatever new ways you conceive, is the desired outcome when it comes to imagination. As King suggests, "The first step to unlocking our imagination is understanding what motivates you."

One of the central elements of the systems that have been created to manage creativity and innovation are standards of measurement — metrics and expertise against which everything is compared. Those elements are what place curbs on our use and application of imagination. Certain professions require those types of standards. Nobody wants a heart surgeon who isn't trained and practiced as a heart surgeon. And nobody wants to fly an airplane that hasn't passed all the necessary safety checks. Being the best at repairing a heart valve or improving the efficiency of a production line will make you an expert in your field. But, as Rita J. King explains, "as soon as you think you're an expert, ask yourself what are you an expert in. Usually you're an expert in navigating a system."

We are living in an unprecedented time in human history. We still need talented surgeons, as well as people who look to improve the way the current systems that power our world function. But, as Rita J. King suggests, as technology and other forces disrupt our society, "we're much more likely to trust someone who doesn't know, but who is willing to find out, than someone who claims to have all the answers. Nobody has dealt with this fast rate of change before, so nobody knows anything for sure anymore." The whole idea of expertise is changing.

By using expertise as the determinant of whether an idea is worth considering or pursuing, we have created a system where you are either in or out, and the value of your imagination is either accepted or not. There is no gray area. As Josh Linkner, an entrepreneur, describes it, "when you have a place where you say 'Hey, let's generate a bunch of really cool ideas and there are no right or wrong answers and everybody wins,'" people will do it. But, if it's "Hey, let's generate a bunch of ideas and if your idea stinks you get fired, and if your idea's the best but it's only one of 100 chance that you get a promotion' then the result is that nobody is going to thrive." Unfortunately, the latter is exactly how the business world is structured.

One of the critical things that is missing, in terms of expertise and leadership, is the idea of challenging how people are thinking about things. Instead, much more emphasis is placed on sharing or promoting existing insights. Our job is to convince others that we are right. True thought leaders help others to generate ideas. They outline a way of thinking and help others to unlock their own insights. The key to unlocking our use of imagination is our willingness to cultivate and push people to think differently.

Thoughtless Acts

What people seem to get confused by most are the differences between innovation and imagination. One day you don't have something, the next you do — that's a product of imagination. Another word that we could use is invention. When there are very incremental steps, and constant updates and improvements to what we already have and know, that is innovation. Most of what we know and experience every day is largely made of old stuff, with a slight tweak having been made, or a slightly different perspective that comes from how you think about things based on your own personal experience or expectations. Innovation is just part of what it takes to lead our lives every day, to make adjustments and find ways to survive as the world around us changes.

The risk with innovation is that we fall into ruts — start to see things only as we have before, or we reasonably expect we should. The responsibility is on to each of us to make sure we constantly look at the world differently, by asking questions, challenging assumptions, and balancing the incremental progress with the possibility of something totally beyond what we believed was possible.

Jane Fulton Siri, the leader of the "human factors" group at IDEO, the international design consultancy, set out to encourage this type of thinking in 2005 in her book *Thoughtless Acts*. By 2005, IDEO was already famous for its approach to designing products and systems that reflected what human beings actually needed — whether we could articulate that need on our own, or simply demonstrated it with our everyday behaviors. IDEO might watch kids brushing their teeth, office workers lining up to board a bus to their office, or patients checking in at the emergency room, trying to find opportunities for design to improve the experience. Their observations led to products including: the first mouse for Apple, a toothpaste tube that made sure no paste was left unused, and an office chair that helped improve worker productivity and reduce injuries, to name a few.

The book invited the reader to notice the subtle and amusing ways that people react to the world around them — and in doing so, inspired the reader to look at the world in entirely different ways. As Fulton Suri explained in an interview, what emerges in the book is the result of a process that pushes the IDEO team to think differently about experiences:

> What type of personality typically makes the best observer? I find that curiosity, open-mindedness, and imagination are important. It helps to be non-judgmental, able to move easily from noticing detail to thinking about patterns and the big picture, perceptive about (their own and other) people's behavior, motivations, and personally genuinely interested in other people's points of reference.[4]

She notes that you need more than objectivity and data to support new ideas and make progress. "It's about people interacting and making decisions and using their creativity. The whole activity is a human one."[5]

In the years since *Thoughtless Acts* was published, IDEO's status as an innovator has only grown and their approach to human-centered design has become a staple of how many organizations think about their work. However, just as innovation has been institutionalized across sectors, the rules and approaches that IDEO, and other design-thinking firms like them, developed have become commonplace and somewhat commoditized.

Kurt Ronn, a creative entrepreneur and philanthropist, cautions that whether the idea is innovation or human-centered design, or anything else that captures our interest, "there is no perfect process or anything, and we would be better off if we taught some basic aspects of how to think." He suggests that common systems are what binds together disparate groups, providing a common language or set of tools that different people, with different experiences or capabilities, can all use in a reasonably similar way. But, he warns that those systems "absolutely blind our ability to see the world in a way different from how we are told, because that one view or approach that we are given gets reinforced by all the people around us." He added, "Our bias is blindness and blindness is our greatest challenge."

The common systems that are developed, and the rules that they impose, encourage us to conform. Moreover, people believe that rules exist to stopping them from taking certain actions, especially trying new and different things. As Kurt Ronn explains, rules should be constantly revisited and revised because what worked for one scenario must be questioned and updated as different needs become clear. "I have ground rules, good questions and rituals, that I could use to tell you how to structure your business, but it really just comes from years and years of knowing when to say 'Wow, that sounds right.'" It may be a cliché to say that rules are meant to be broken, but in this case it is true — and necessary. Using and applying our imagination is one of the ways that we can identify what rules need to be challenged.

"I think there are industries where you have to follow the rules very specifically," explains Peter Shankman, the founder and CEO of The Geek Factory, Inc., a boutique Social Media, Marketing and PR Strategy firm. "If you work in a plant that makes cars and you have a very specific job to do and you start using your imagination to create a different car you are probably not going to work there for very long." But, Shankman suggests there are plenty of times where you can use your imagination even within those situations — and while they might not have an immediate impact, they do contribute to the overall culture of the organization. "There is nothing that should stop you from saying 'Hey, boss, I have a better idea about how to do this'," offered Shankman. "There's nothing wrong with that, as long as that culture exists and the boss is open to listening." Increasingly, companies that don't allow for that sort of conversation to happen, or for employees — regardless of their position in the organization — to use and apply their imagination — are the ones that fail.

But for the rest of us, closing the gap means opening up every other possible options that we haven't yet considered. Instead of being instructed to think in a particular way, or follow a set of clearly defined steps, Shankman believes "we should be giving people the space to explore, and learn through that experience. It won't come from sitting in a room thinking deep thoughts; it's much more holistic and practical in terms of finding it."

In other words, we will need to use our imagination to close the imagination gap.

Asking Questions

According to a study by British retailer Littlewoods.com, children ask an average of about 300 questions a day. Four-year-old girls are the most curious, asking about 390 questions per day. Nine-year-old boys are the least, asking just 144 questions per day. Between breakfast and tea time, the average mother faced roughly one question every two-and-a-half minutes. While the number of questions that children ask falls with age, the questions they ask increase in difficulty.[6]

When children ask questions, they are generating new and different inputs and allowing their brains to make sense of the world around them. Children ask the same questions over and over again because as they experience more and gain new perspective, they need to go back and reconsider what they have learned. But over time, most kids stop asking so many questions. As Po Bronson and Ashley Merryman wrote in *Newsweek*, "Preschool children, on average, ask their parents about 100 questions a day. Why, why, why – sometimes parents just wish it'd stop. Tragically, it does stop. By middle school they've pretty much stopped asking. It's no coincidence that this same time is when student motivation and engagement plummet. They didn't stop asking questions because they lost interest: it's the other way around. They lost interest because they stopped asking questions."[7] We stop asking questions because we become afraid of the answers (or the reaction to even asking the question). We stop asking questions because we don't receive the same incentives we did when we were younger — we get rewarded for giving correct answers, not being curious about new subjects. We stop asking questions because we discover that asking questions opens us up to judgment and risk.

Questions are how we learn and gain perspective, not just when we are young, but throughout our lives. If you don't ask questions, we will not introduce as much new information into our brains, and we won't feed your imagination as much. Closing the imagination gap will require us to ask more questions.

Challenge: Ask Crazy Questions

ParentsTogether is a national nonprofit organization that provides resources, connections, and community that help all kids and parents thrive. One of their signature programs, Q4KIDZ, sends parents a daily fun, creative question via text message to spark conversation with kids. Questions include:

If you could go back in time, what modern technology would you take with you? How do you think they would react?

If you could make any two people in all of history meet, who would you introduce to one another? Why?

If you were told that you could be invisible for an entire day, what would you do and where would you go?

If you could give your pet (or favorite animal) any super power, what would that super power be and why?

What would you do if you came home to a band of goats playing instruments in your living room?

Imagine everyone walked on the ceiling instead of the ground, how would life be different?

Imagine you are given a remote that rewinds, fast-forwards, and pauses time. What would you do with this remote? Would you tell anyone you have it?

If you could make any person in the world super silly for a day, who would you pick?

To Do: Every day, once a day, ask someone a truly silly question. If you need inspiration, sign up for Q4KIDZ.

NOTES

1. The MIT Press; Reprint edition, October 20, 1994.
2. https://hbr.org/2012/05/please-can-we-all-just-stop-innovating
3. Schumpeter, J. *Capitalism, Socialism, and Democracy*, 1942, p. 83.
4. Q&A with Jane Fulton Siri — Creative Generalist. http://creativegeneralist.blogspot.com/2006/11/creative-generalist-qa-jane-fulton.html

5. http://hci.stanford.edu/dschool/resources/needfinding/fulton_suri_thoughtless_acts.pdf
6. http://www.dailymail.co.uk/femail/article-2300833/How-mothers-field-288-questions-day-Answer-questions-hour-David-Cameron-Prime-Minister-s-Questions.html
7. http://www.newsweek.com/creativity-crisis-74665

Imagination and Language (Framing, Expectations)

> ### 5

Language has always been vital to the development of culture. It changes to reflect new concepts and different technologies. Closing the Imagination Gap will require a new way of talking about the challenges that we face and what is both possible and realistic to achieve. This chapter explores how shifting the framing of the issues and challenges, and setting new expectations, will spark new uses of our imagination.

Everything starts with an idea. Sometimes, all we have is an idea and nothing more. That idea might be shared; it could influence how people think, or inspire someone to take action. But it exists solely as an idea, a concept, and a thought. In other cases, an idea is used to create something real — a product, a policy, a business. It's in the process of turning an idea into something real that things get complicated, and where the language we use, and what that does to shape our understanding matters most.

According to researchers at the University of Haifa, original ideas — novel solutions to problems — have value.[1] If the idea is not fully applicable it is considered unreasonable. In other words, only ideas that we know what to do with should be considered.

I disagree. Let's take a deeper look at the research.

The researchers hypothesized that to form new ideas the brain must activate a number of different — and perhaps even contradictory — networks. In the first part of the research, respondents were asked to come up with new, original, and unexpected ideas for how to use different objects. Answers that were provided infrequently received a high score for originality, while those given frequently received a lower score. In the second part, respondents were asked to provide their best description of the objects. During the tests, scanners measured brain activity while the subjects provided the answers.

The researchers found increased brain activity in an "associative" region among participants whose originality was high. This region mainly works in the background when a person is not concentrating, similar to daydreaming. But they also found that this region did not operate alone when an original answer was given. For the answer to be original, an additional region, the administrative control region (a more "conservative" region related to social norms and rules) worked in collaboration with the associative region. The researchers also found that the stronger the connection (i.e., the better these regions work together in parallel), the greater the level of originality of the answer.[2]

Wait a second. The research proved that our most compelling concepts, the ones that haven't considered before, emerge from the part of the brain that is prone to wild thoughts and so-called unreasonable ideas. But the analysis suggested that the ideas that deserve to be celebrated are the ones that we think make sense, because they connect to our own personal experience. Those two perspectives are at odds with each other.

The challenge here is not with the science — it is important to have evidence to show that different parts of the brain contribute to the formation of different types of ideas. The problem is with the framing and language. The basic hypothesis is biased. The scientists preassigned a value to the ideas that were offered by the subjects in the experiment based on the idea's utility. That completely changes the meaning and consideration, and ultimately influences the results. Instead of talking about where ideas come from, these scientists have established a qualification system for ideas — and one that is particularly dangerous when it comes to imagination.

As previous chapters have outlined, imagination is about invention and fostering new thinking and ideas, while creativity and innovation are applied in more practical and measurable ways. That distinction is important for many reasons: first, they are different — imagination comes before creativity and innovation, it feeds those processes. Second, how are we to know what ideas are valuable or not before they are fully considered? Are we to believe that something that at its first introduction seems impractical — or in the words of the researchers from Haifa University, "unreasonable" — should not be further considered. Think about what our society would look like today if we had succeeded in deeming ideas like electricity, human genomics, space travel, and more as unreasonable, and not worthy of further consideration? There is no scientific analysis of the functioning of the brain that should ever be put in a position to form that judgment. As the research above clearly demonstrates, the words we use will determine whether imagination will be given a chance at all.

Words Influence Behaviors

The choices we make as individuals — how we spend our time, what we support, our willingness to commit or sacrifice, and more — depend on our ability to understand and appreciate the impact the choice will have on our lives. That understanding is derived from the language that is used to present the options under consideration. If we want someone to embrace your idea you have to explain the benefits. We have to prove that our information deserves to make it through their filter. This is especially challenging when it comes to the application of imagination because whatever your brain has offered up is not going to be something that others have necessarily experienced. And without that experience or context, the words you use to describe something may not make sense to someone else.

There is an overwhelming desire in many of us to make things better — to change how the world functions so that we, and everyone else, can benefit. But if that call for change is not presented well, if the expectations are not aligned with what people want, it won't happen. Think about our efforts to promote conservation, voter participation, or disaster preparedness. Full participation would deliver benefits to not only the individual, but also the community more broadly; however, people do not take it upon themselves to turn off the water, show up at the polls, or make an emergency plan because they don't appreciate the impact of their actions.

In 2010, TrendWatching, one of the leading global trend firms, outlined a list of 10 "Crucial Consumer Trends"[3] for the year ahead. The first of those ideas they titled "Business as Unusual" and suggested we lower our expectations for change. They wrote:

> Prepare for "business as unusual." For the first time, there's a global understanding, if not a feeling of urgency that sustainability, in every possible meaning of the word, is the only way forward. How that should or shouldn't impact consumer societies is of course still part of a raging debate, but at least there is a debate.

> Meanwhile, in mature consumer societies, companies will have to do more than just embrace the notion of being a good corporate citizen. To truly prosper, they will have to "move with the culture." This may mean displaying greater transparency and honesty, or having conversations as opposed to one-way advertising, or championing collaboration instead of an us-them mentality. Or, it could be intrinsically about generosity versus greed, or being a bit edgy and daring as opposed to safe and bland.

In other words, we shouldn't expect to change things — even in our hyper-connected, everyone-can-launch-a-movement, technology-enabled society. Why should we resign ourselves to a slow, painful reality of seeing organizations of all types fail to change and meet our expectations? Wouldn't a better option be to redouble our efforts to make things happen, and commit to telling whoever will listen, through every means at our disposal — buying power, political action, media commentary, and more — that slow, insufficient change and more business as usual is not going to work?

Unfortunately, most people are willing to accept what an organization like TrendWatching says is inevitable. When people hear that there was little chance of things changing, they shut off their imagination and they go along. But it doesn't have to be that way. Just as TrendWatching can convince people that we are all doomed, any organization or person can use their words to influence how we think and act in ways that will make change. They can provide us with ideas and concepts, feed our imagination, and encourage us to make those ideas our own and generate new plans and opportunities.

Jake Siewert knows a thing or two about how words can be used to shape thinking and influence perceptions. He worked on the 1992 Presidential election campaign and later served as Press Secretary in the White House during the Clinton Administration. He now leads corporate communications for Goldman Sachs. He told me "the only way something really takes hold is if someone has an idea. And that idea has to resonate. If they're somewhat passionate about the new idea and become an evangelist for that idea, they can get that idea adopted. Why? Because people will begin to believe 'That's interesting. I'd like to try that or do that'."[4] Siewert explained that words can have influence regardless of the setting — as long as the message and context are aligned.

Between the time he left the White House and began working at Goldman Sachs, Siewert worked at Alcoa, the aluminum-manufacturing giant. Siewert says that Paul O'Neill, when he first became CEO of Alcoa in 1987, proved the influence of words on behavior. Their investors were nervous because Alcoa was trying to recover from some failed product ideas and other problems. But O'Neill didn't talk about profit margins, revenue projections, or anything else that would be comforting to Wall Street. In his first speech as CEO, he took a very different approach:

> I want to talk to you about worker safety. Every year, numerous Alcoa workers are injured so badly that they miss a day of work. Our safety record is better than the

general American workforce, especially considering that our employees work with metals that are 1500 degrees and machines that can rip a man's arm off. But it's not good enough. I intend to make Alcoa the safest company in America. I intend to go for zero injuries.

Even at Alcoa, a traditional manufacturing company, Siewert told me "Paul O'Neill had this idea anyone who comes to work should know that they're going to go home at the end of the day and be safe with their families in the same way that they would if they were going to an office. He was super passionate about that." O'Neill shared his idea — an entirely safe workplace for all employees — at every opportunity. "It was really the passion of his vision around a zero-incident workplace that made the difference. There was lots of jargon. But his point was clear. You should go home safe if you work in a manufacturing industry. It should be no different than if you're going into the office." And it worked. Alcoa became one of the safest industrial companies in the country and worker productivity improved. Wall Street responded positively as well.

O'Neill drove that vision home over a number of years, and even after he left, it didn't fall apart. "People had been animated by this idea, and the explanation he offered, and they adopted it. It wasn't adopting it because there was some checkmark that they had to do or some bonus they received. There were a lot of things that Alcoa developed that were more successful to the bottom line, but it was because the words he used, the passion it sparked, and the impact it had on the business overall that this example is so important. The vision really caught people, and that really takes hold."

Importantly, the vision that Paul O'Neill was promoting across Alcoa was not based on data or introduced with a financial rationale in mind. He didn't say he wanted the company to be slightly safer (or slightly less dangerous) than it has been in the past. O'Neill introduced the idea of a zero incident workplace — "which for a manufacturing company was probably as ambitious as putting a man on the moon. And had it not been suggested by the highest ranking person in the company, it probably would have been dismissed before it even was given a chance to succeed." The words he used and the way he framed the idea inspired people inside and outside the company to use their imagination, to believe in a completely safe workplace, and the shifts in behavior followed.

Jake Siewert believes that "lasting change – whether it's inside a company or in politics – starts with someone who is selling a vision and getting voluntary adoption. If they're trying to force it on people it doesn't work. It just won't work. There are a lot of politicians with conviction that their idea is the best. But politicians ... they don't all succeed," Siewert noted. "The ones who succeed are the ones who manage to capture people's imagination by communicating their vision of how the world can be a little bit better. That's very different than the way business operates." There will always be businesses that succeed at making a profit without doing anything new or bold. There will be people who can hold the attention of a crowd and paint a rosy picture of the future, but don't deliver on the promise. The most influential organizations will always be those that combine those elements, by using imagination to inspire and push new thinking and then pursue those ideas, create new products (or solutions, or anything), and realize growth and success as a result.

Moonshots

Which crazy, imaginative ideas get embraced and which get dismissed? How do we know if something is truly new and different — or just the next logical step (or two, or three) ahead in the world we already live? A lot of it has to do with how the idea is presented. The words and images we use to describe the idea either elevate it to something of seemingly limitless opportunity, or position it as disruptive, but still recognizable.

In 1961, just six weeks after the Soviet Union's Yuri Gagarin became the first human to reach space, President Kennedy spoke to an audience of 40,000 people in the football stadium at Rice University in Houston, Texas. In his speech, he said "This nation should commit itself to achieving the goal, before the decade is out, of landing a man on the moon and returning him safely to the Earth." The concept of *moonshot* entered the lexicon as shorthand for "a difficult or expensive task, the outcome of which is expected to have great significance."[5]

Scott D. Anthony and Mark Johnson, from Innosight, a future-oriented business consulting firm, explained in *Harvard Business Review* that a good moonshot has three ingredients. First, it inspires. Second, it is credible. And finally, they wrote "it is imaginative. It isn't an obvious extrapolation of what's happening today (which for Kennedy would simply have been to fly farther into space), but something that offers a meaningful break from the past."

President Kennedy's "moonshot" speech was inspiring, credible — and certainly imaginative. As the President explained at the time:

> We choose to go to the moon. We choose to go to the moon in this decade and do the other things, not because they are easy, but because they are hard, because that goal will serve to organize and measure the best of our energies and skills, because that challenge is one that we are willing to accept, one we are unwilling to postpone, and one which we intend to win, and the others, too.

The federal government did indeed make Apollo a national priority, pouring an estimated $25 billion (well over $100 billion in today's money) into the program over the next several years (*Note: in 1966, NASA funding represented 4.4% of the federal budget, compared with less than 0.5% in 2015*). And in 1969, the United States successfully met President Kennedy's challenge and put a man on the moon.

Until the early 1960s, when President Kennedy challenged Americans to put a man on the moon, there was no phrase to describe these types of ideas. In the decades since, it seems every globally ambitious concept is assigned the title of moonshot — from every XPrize nominee to the more recent White House Task Force on Curing Cancer.

Astro Teller, the head of Google X, the division within the tech giant that is exclusively focused on pursuing big, imaginative projects, describes moonshots as follows:

> Moonshot thinking starts with picking a big problem: something huge, long existing, or on a global scale. Next it involves articulating a radical solution — one that would actually solve the problem if it existed: a product or service that sounds like it's directly out of a sci-fi story. Finally there needs to be some kind of concrete evidence that the proposed solution is not quite as crazy as it at first seems; something that justifies at least a close look at whether such a solution could be brought into being if enough creativity, passion, and persistence were brought to bear on it. This evidence could be some breakthrough in science, technology, or engineering that could actually make the solution possible within the next decade or so.[6]

Teller adds that "without all three of these things, you may have a sci-fi story or a crazy idea — but you don't have a moonshot. Not one that can aim for new heights and address a big challenge in a maybe-not-*totally*-crazy kind of way."

Google X was established in early 2010 specifically to "identify and implement once-impossible sci-fi fantasies: Hail Mary projects like the self-driving car. Or Google Glass, a wearable computing system. Or an artificial brain, in which a cluster of computers running advanced algorithms learn from the world around them, much like humans do."[7] Of course, those specific ideas don't seem so ridiculous today, since Google and others (Tesla, Apple, etc.) went out and made them happen. The idea of pushing for new concepts still drives a lot of thinking and exploration in business, and especially technology startups.

Larry Page, the cofounder of Google, was inspired to shoot for the moon — if you will — while an undergrad at the University of Michigan. He had become involved with a student leadership-training program called LeaderShape which preached "a healthy disregard for the impossible." That inspiration prompted him, along with Sergey Brin, to create Google and build a company with a healthy appreciation for the value of imagination. In a Q&A for *Wired* magazine, Larry Page was asked about that inspiration, and how it continues to inform Google's ambitions:

> I worry that something has gone seriously wrong with the way we run companies. If you read the media coverage of our company, or of the technology industry in general, it's always about the competition. The stories are written as if they are covering a sporting event. But it's hard to find actual examples of really amazing things that happened solely due to competition. How exciting is it to come to work if the best you can do is trounce some other company that does roughly the same thing? That's why most companies decay slowly over time. They tend to do approximately what they did before, with a few minor changes. It's natural for people to want to work on things that they know aren't going to fail. But incremental improvement is guaranteed to be obsolete over time. Especially in technology, where you know there's going to be non-incremental change [because of the constantly increasing speed and power of computer processors, the availability of the cloud and more].

> So a big part of my job is to get people focused on things that are not just incremental. Take Gmail. When we released that, we were a search company—it was a leap for us to put out an email product, let alone one that gave users 100 times as much storage as they could get anywhere else. That is not something that would have happened naturally if we had been focusing on incremental improvements.

When asked why there aren't more people with the kind of ambition that you see at Google, Page acknowledged that truly big, ambitious, and new ideas are hard to come by. "It's not easy coming up with moon shots. And we're not teaching people how to identify those difficult projects," he offered. "Where would I go to school to learn what kind of technological programs I should work on? You'd probably need a pretty broad technical education and some knowledge about organization and entrepreneurship. There's no degree for that. Our system trains people in specialized ways, but not to pick the right projects to make a broad technological impact." While there are people who are using and applying their imagination, there is no clear path or pipeline for a company like Google to identify those people, or surface those ideas.[8]

Nobody knows exactly what is written on the Google X white board right now and the specific ideas matter all that much. One thing we do know is that the moonshot projects that Google pursues are some of the most expensive the company invests in. According to *the New York Times*, "Alphabet's second-quarter earnings report ... showed an operating loss of $859 million in Other Bets" — the line item where Google X is listed.[9] To think of it another way, Google's quarterly loss exceeds the annual revenue of many companies in the United States. No matter though, because profit is not what drives Google X, and their success (or lack of success) should not weigh too heavily on our thinking. What is important is that what Google X says, and does, and how they think, can inspire more people to embrace their imagination and have a little bit of the same ambition that fuels Google's efforts forward.

How We Should Approach Things

How we frame a problem creates the environment within which you get to operate. If you don't choose the right problem or don't choose an interesting enough problem then that's going to color everything after that. "There are all kinds of ways you can get at those problems," explains Marty Neumeier, the Director of

Transformation at Liquid Agency. Neumeier told me that when he puts together workshops with clients and partners designed to push new ideas and thinking, he always features a mixture of people, some who self-identify as having more of an imagination than others, some who self-diagnose as having no imagination at all. Working together they are able to offer up really new concepts. "Normally you get a group together and everyone shoots down everyone else's ideas and everyone goes away feeling bad or they come up with something good but then there's no follow through. But there's ways of working around that."[10] Neumeier says it is all about changing the focus of the conversation.

> When someone has a problem to solve they think back to what they learned in school or what they read about in the *Harvard Business Review*. Or maybe they try to draw on what they did at their last company that worked. People are always looking for something in the past to apply, some principle, and then they immediately go for it and they never make a move that's very bold because they know that's inherently risky. What they need to be doing is imagining something, making a prototype, taking that prototype and bending it to do something cool that's never be done, testing it, see if it works.
>
> What that does is push back in two ways. It pushes back on what you know because suddenly you know something you didn't know. You've got an idea that wasn't on the table before. It also pushes against what you're going to do too because suddenly that thing you were going to do before looks pretty ineffectual compared to the thing you could do that you just saw, that thing you invented.

Bradley Feinstein, a tech entrepreneur and the cofounder of Dropel Fabrics, says there is only one question that is required to change the conversation: "Why?" He notes that kids ask the question at a very early age, because it helps them to make sense of the world around them. "And it would have the same impact if it was used more often today, because it would encourage us to question the norms, to ask why it is that we're doing something the way that we do something just because that's the way we do it," Feinstein told me. "You don't need to reinvent the wheel every time, but there are instances where reinventing the wheel can change the world. That's why I love that question, I love the question "Why?"[11]

Importantly, Feinstein says the goal of asking that question is not to generate a specific, right answer. "There can't be a right answer to a question that we haven't asked before," he explained. "Instead, asking is about understanding how you think, the steps that you're taking to solve a problem, sometimes strategically and sometimes not."

Write the Story

There are hundreds of different types of games we can play — alone, with friends or colleagues, or with children. Every one of them will find a way to trigger your imagination. When someone pushes a metal thimble around the Monopoly board, they are transformed into an early 20th century real estate baron. A game of Candyland routinely provokes discussion about how different choices (caramel instead of gumdrops for example) would change the board setup (as my daughter noted recently, caramel is much stickier so there would be more lose-a-turn options). Even dice baseball, the playing of which requires only that someone roll a dice and translate the number that is displayed into a walk, hit, or strike out. If you play with my son, the game always includes a comprehensive play-by-play description with enough detail and commentary involved, if you were to overhear it from the next room you would think you had stumbled onto a broadcast of Vic Scully calling a Dodgers game on the radio.

The games we play are built around a specific challenge or a fundamental competition. There are winners and losers to be declared or achievements to be unlocked. The game isn't officially over until time runs out, or some milestone has been achieved. In other words, most games are not primarily designed to trigger your imagination, but that is what happens when you play.

There are some games that are primarily designed to trigger your imagination. One such game, Tell Me A Story, is produced by a New York–based children's toy company and design studio called eeBoo. It features a set of 36 sturdy, laminated story cards adorned with different illustrations. We have the Robot's Mission set (they also sell Mystery in the Forest, Circus Animal Adventure, and other themes). One purpose to the game is to use the cards to tell a story. The promotional materials on the company website say that "Children can use them individually, parents can use them, or play groups can build stories together."

We have played Tell Me A Story dozens of times — spreading the cards out on the floor in our apartment, organizing and reorganizing them depending on who was sharing their version of the tale this time. No two stories have ever been even remotely similar, and in most cases the tales we spin out are so far from the reality of our everyday lives that the origins of the idea — other than the drawing provided on the cards — are impossible to trace back to anything but our imagination.

Each time we finish playing — whether the game consumed our attention for an hour, or stretched across several days (and several rooms), the cards get piled back up and returned to their box. I don't recall any of the stories we crafted and even seeing the cards when they next emerge does little to prompt my memory. Whatever came out of our imaginations seems to have gone away — we enjoyed ourselves, but nothing came of it.

Why do we allow the ideas that emerge to be forgotten? As ideas emerge and new possibilities for how games should be played — or entirely new ways of seeing the world flood out of our brain — why aren't we capturing them? We should be writing them down.

"J.K. Rowling and J.R. Tolkien both created worlds using the tools of words that we've inhabited," Bryan Johnson, an entrepreneur and investor, told me. "As entrepreneurs, we have the ability to author our existence — the products we build, the people we hire, the culture we create, our very reason for existence."[12] Arguably, entrepreneurs have always held this special type of influence, because of their incredible power to create, or to author, the future.

Bryan Johnson has invested in dozens of companies, all of them in one way or another designed to create tools that will determine what kind of world we build in the coming decades and centuries. He gravitates toward investing in projects that are designed to have a long-term benefit, or establish a platform from which other new opportunities might emerge because he knows, from experience, how challenging it is to not just conceive of big ideas, but to pursue them. More straightforward investments that are likely to provide a quick return might make him money, but their impact won't be as great. He believes the long-term potential for bold ideas to shape the future is much more compelling and important.

When we choose to qualify ideas as big versus small or say that they improve versus disrupt something, we impose a prejudgment that has significant influence over the potential for the idea to gain traction. But the broader public, with so many different competing interests and options for how to spend their time or invest their resources, will be quick to dismiss something if there is even one small thing that does not align with their existing opinions, beliefs, or values. It is easier to just follow the pack and only focus our interests on ideas that have some guarantee of success — but that doesn't make it the best decision.

"I would argue that we need to be less lazy," Rita J. King told me. "Our brains are amazing, but they are also lazy, in a way, because they need to conserve energy to help us survive. That impacts us, and society, in ways we don't realize." She said this laziness is one of the explanations for why sexism, racism, and ageism continue to persist, arguing that many people are just relying on heuristics that the brain uses to file categories, without even realizing that they're doing it. Complex social dynamics are of less interest to our brains than things like access to food and water. The same logic explains why people buy pink and blue gifts depending on the gender of a new baby. "It's not because we consciously want to perpetuate gender stereotypes, it's because our brains are trying to conserve energy by only focusing on critical things. If you're shopping for a present for a boy, it's easier to grab something off the blue shelf because you've been bombarded with the message that blue equals boy. Your brain doesn't need to waste energy second guessing that because it doesn't perceive the issue as critical to survival." If our brains are lazy, you can expect the rest of our behaviors to be impacted as well. If we think voting doesn't matter, we won't make the effort to go to the polls. If we think that someone else will take care of a problem that challenges our society, we won't make a donation or commit our energy. And if that laziness becomes commonplace in our society, it will be harder to drive change.

Mental Blocks

Our default setting as humans is to think that difficult things are impossible — until proven otherwise. But if we believe something can happen, it's only a matter of time before it does.

This phenomenon in our thinking is known as "The Bannister Effect" — named for Roger Bannister, who on May 6, 1954, ran the first sub-four-minute mile. His 3.59.4 time was the fastest time ever recorded (*Note: running has been a competitive sport since Ancient Greece, but only officially recorded for roughly a half-century at the time*) and broke a record that nobody thought was humanly possible to beat. Two months later, Bannister raced his rival John Landy of Australia and won that race, with both men going under four minutes. Within three years 16 more runners had recorded a sub-four-minute mile. Today, the "four-minute barrier" is the standard of all male professional middle distance runners and in the last 60 years, the mile record has been lowered by almost 17 seconds.[13]

Does imagining a faster mile time make it possible to break that record? Yes. Not on its own, of course. But Roger Bannister and his coaches believed that they could run faster — they imagined the possibility of achieving a record time — and they set to work to make it happen. Once the mental limitations were lifted, everything changed — everyone's imagination started to spin off ideas and possibilities related to running faster.

Imagination paved the way. The small group that believed provided the proof that the rest of the world needed to think differently about the challenge. "Lots of technology is involved in the new things we are discovering and achieving – and the technology gets a lot of the credit," Sree Sreenivasan told me. "But, it's really about overcoming the mental blocks. I think the four-minute mile is the best example because there was no technology involved."[14]

Sreenivasan said the Bannister Effect was very much a factor in his work with the Metropolitan Museum of Art, particularly when presenting the museum's content in new and different formats. "One of the leaps of imagination was to say that our audience loves the content but they hate the format," meaning that to enjoy the Met's collection you had to visit the museum in New York City, walk through the corridors, and read the written descriptions for each artifact. "We asked ourselves, 'what would happen if we put all our content online free for the world to have?' So that's what we did, and today anybody in the world on their phone, no app required, can watch and listen and hear our 2600 audio stops, which is an example of something that no one would set out to do." Sreenivasan noted that many people within the organization simply couldn't imagine how to overcome the practical challenges of posting all the content online.

The Met, like so many other cultural institutions today, charges museum visitors for listening devices that can be carried around the museum to supplement a visitor's experience viewing the art. If everyone was given free access to the content, the thinking went, visitors would no longer rent the devices when they visit in person, and that would undermine an important source of revenue for the organization. But that wasn't actually what happened. The experiment yielded some interesting results: "It turns out there are two different audiences. So far the data is looking really good, that the foreign tourist wants to come, they don't want to worry about charging their device, they just want to pull out their phone and they listen to it. Whereas the New Yorkers here, they don't want to then retrace their steps and get to the front hall, rent the device and then come back. They just pull out their phone and they listen to the information."

For Sreenivasan and his team, creating the audio drops and making them available online was one small part of their quest to imagine the Met's content in new and different ways. Making the audio available to a broader audience, including translating it into more languages, would serve to further the museum's goal of attracting a larger and increasingly diverse global audience. But even with hard evidence showing that audiences enjoyed the audio wanted to access it in their own language, some people across the museum's leadership were still not able to get around their existing mental blocks. He explained that the existing line of thinking was deeply embedded into the museum's practices. "The British Museum has 200 audio stops, 80 percent translated into multiple different languages. The Louvre has 960 audio messages, 100 percent translated. We have 2600 audio stops, but just one percent translated. What do you think we need — more messages or more languages? We need more languages. What do you think the curators want to do? More messages." The curators' experience, and their focus, is on how to present as many pieces of content as possible — they struggle to imagine what the audience might want, and what could enhance their experience.

Sreenivasan, who describes his position at the Met as running, "a 70-person startup inside a 145-year-old company" faces two challenges at the same time. His department is tasked with helping visitors feel that the museum is accessible, while also pushing the organization internally to change its approach to better suit modern times. "A lot of people just can't imagine us doing things any other way than we do now," Sreenivasan told me. "They can't visualize what it might look like if don't a different way."

Sebastian Buckup, the head of programming for the World Economic Forum, says that science fiction has played an important role in the progression of history and our conception of a new future.[15] He uses examples including Mary Shelley's *Frankenstein,* *Star Wars, Star Trek,* and *Alien* to illustrate how science fiction has both inspired some of our best, most innovative thinking and given rise to our worst fears and behaviors as a society. "By imaginatively combining the rigor of science with the freedom of fiction, the genre plays a big role in expressing the hopes and fears we project into our creations," he explains.

Buckup also explains the best sci-fi stories mix two ingredients.

The first is great science which sometimes leads to surprising accuracy: Jules Verne imagined a propeller-driven aircraft in the early 19th century, when balloons were the best that aviation had to offer. In the 1960s, Arthur C. Clarke envisioned the iPad, and Ray Bradbury the Mars landing. It may just be a matter of time until "Samantha", the AI voice in Spike Jonze's film *Her,* will be real, or until we bump into a version of *Ava,* the humanoid robot from Alex Garland's *Ex Machina.*

The second ingredient is a keen understanding of contemporary hopes and fears. This is what makes these books and films great tools for dissecting the sentiments of an era. The two most successful sci-fi stories ever, George Lucas' Star Wars and Gene Roddenberry's Star Trek, are amongst the best examples of how pop culture combined perceptions of technological progress with contemporary hopes and fears.

While there are plenty of examples of dramatic advancements in science and technology, and the economic benefits that followed, Buckup says that more recently we have failed to advance as far, or as fast, as seems possible, or as science suggest we should have. "The defining feature of our days is that we feel like we live in an era of incredibly innovation, mostly thanks to staggering breakthroughs in science and technology; but, at the same time, we feel like there are insurmountable limits in the form of economic, political and environmental risks." Buckup goes on to urge us to embrace imagination, not as sci-fi enthusiasts, but as citizens and leaders, writing:

> Dreams can make us go out and spend, start businesses and build factories; but they can also put fear in our hearts, make us lock our doors and save our resources. They can blind us from reality and cover up political horror but also inspire us to great achievements. "Longing on a large scale is what makes history," writes novelist Don DeLillo.

> Our real challenge is not the proverbial fight between man and machine, recounted so many times since the Luddite era. It is on the one hand the struggle against cynicism and apathy, the toxic by-products of trust that were squandered in the crises of our decade; on the other, it is the struggle with prophets who promise that technology will solve all problems. On both ends, it is the struggle with a technological discourse that discounts our ability to shape a better future; a discourse that makes us passive subjects in a world of volatility, uncertainty, complexity and ambiguity.

The critical factor in all this is our imagination, and how we apply it to the shaping of the future that we want to see, or believe is necessary.

The Thinking Photographer

The concept of pre-visualization in photography is where the photographer can see the final print before the image has been captured. Though he was not the first to talk about the preparations a photographer must make to ensure a successful image is made, Ansel Adams is widely credited with defining and explaining the importance of visualization. In his first book,

Modern Photography, 1934—35: The Studio Annual of Camera Art, Adams wrote:

> The camera makes an image-record of the object before it. It records the subject in terms of the optical properties of the lens, and the chemical and physical properties of the negative and print. The control of that record lies in the selection by the photographer and in his understanding of the photographic processes at his command. The photographer visualizes his conception of the subject as presented in the final print. He achieves the expression of his visualization through his technique—aesthetic, intellectual, and mechanical.

And in his Autobiography, he expanded on this idea:

> Visualization is not simply choosing the best filter. To be fully achieved it does require a good understanding of both the craft and aesthetics of photography ... The visualization of a photograph involves the intuitive search for meaning, shape, form, texture, and the projection of the image-format on the subject. The image forms in the mind—is visualized—and another part of the mind calculates the physical processes involved in determining the exposure and development of the image of the negative and anticipates the qualities of the final print. The creative artist is constantly roving the worlds without, and creating new worlds within.[16]

Ansel Adams was talking about imagination, and the ways that photographers must use their imagination in their work. "Pre-visualization is imagination" Jamie Rose, an award-winning photographer and the co-founder of Momenta Group, told me before reeling off a series of questions that she counsels new and experienced photographers alike to consider when setting up for a shoot. "Why don't we do it that way? Wouldn't it be great if we could take a photograph that looks like this? What is the purpose of the image and who is going to look at it? How am I going to frame it and what camera settings do I need to capture the idea? Making a good photograph requires more than a good camera or being in the right place at the right time."[17] The Momenta Group trains creatives to work with nonprofit organizations as a sustainable revenue stream and operates a creatives services firm which works with international for-profit and non-profit clients. Rose says that photographer will always put his or her own personal perspective and talents into an image, and, more than anything, "that requires imagination."

The same concept of pre-visualization applies to acting. Sarah Stiles, who was nominated for Tony Award for her work in *Hand to God* told me "my work is 80–90% imagination. There are other words we use — we talk about particularization a lot, the idea of recalling things that have happened to you that are similar or give you the same emotion that a character needs at a certain point, even if it's not the same situation exactly." Stiles said an actor can then put himself or herself back in that place, imagining that they are talking to that person with those circumstances and drawing on those authentic feelings, but repurposing them.

For most roles, the actor hasn't been through what their character might be experiencing, challenging the actor to imagine themselves in a situation, as well as the backstory that contributed to the makeup of the character. "For my role in *Hand to God* (in which she plays Jessica, a teenage member of a Christian puppet theatre group at a church in small-town Texas), I have imagined what a day in her life looks like from when she was a little girl until now. What are all the things that have happened to her to bring her to this point in the story? You do a whole background analysis – but in your head. When I get a script, I spend a lot of time imagining, and visualizing, those different scenarios."[18]

There is no universal process that actors are told to follow — each role, each person playing that role, crafts an approach that works for them. There is Method Acting, the Meisner Approach, Practical Aesthetics, and more. In every case, however, "you start with the basics. You start with what the script gives you," explains Stiles. "How old is she? Where is she from? Who are her parents? Whatever information the script can actually give you." For the role of Jessica, for which Stiles was nominated for the Tony Award, there wasn't information available in the script. "We actually didn't even know her age. We know that her dad picks her up, so she's not driving, but that could be because she doesn't have a car. But we decided she was somewhere around 15 or 16 from that. We know that she's from Texas. We know that she and (one of the other characters), Timmy had some sort of history. But that's really it." The rest, Stiles told me, she had to make real for herself.

"I tend to start with the physicality because that really helps me feel who she is. Jessica is very grounded — she's the voice of reason in the play. So, I felt immediately that there was this still-ness about her. This person who is very secure and grounded in herself, what does that mean about how she was brought up? What would a person that has that kind of intelligence and that sort of creative way of thinking that shows in how she gets out of the situations, the way she can connect with (the show's main character) Jason — what does that tell me? I also think about why they cast me? There must be something about me that what they saw. In the room they saw this girl — there are things about me that felt right for Jessica, so what are those things from my child-hood that I can twist and turn and make real for her too?"

Stiles looks at each of the nuggets of information she learns, or imagines, about a character as a puzzle piece. "Being an actress — you get all these little puzzles that lead you to other places and from there your character emerges." And when the audience sees that, even without access to the script or an extended conversation with the actress playing the role on stage, they are able to under-stand the story — and to share in her imagination.

One of the basic functions of imagination is the formation of mental images, as a way of taking an idea or concept and helping a person to make sense of it in relation to their real life. Our imagination automatically creates visuals to help supple-ment our reality — we can appreciate the stove is hot without touching it, or anticipate that a car might turn the corner prompting us to look both ways before crossing the street. More importantly, by using and applying our imagination actively, we can create new images — make up entire personas of characters we play, or think through options before snapping a picture. The more we use those powers to visualize, the more powerful our imagination becomes.

Overcoming Resistance

When you check into a hotel you are likely to find a sign, maybe on the counter in your bathroom or affixed to the mirror above the sink, that encourages you to reuse bath towels during your stay. The message is designed to communicate the hotel's interest in helping the environment by committing to a reduction in their water use. If you agree, you will hang your towels for reuse. If you don't agree, either with the hotel's message, or the general concept of environmental sustainability, you will leave the towels to be cleaned daily.

While an estimated 85% of hotels have a reuse program in place, guest participation is mediocre at best. The problem lies in the messaging. The hotels try to appeal to guests to help the hotel save energy, to save the environment, or conserve resources. But messages that focus on the issue or cause don't work as well as those that seek to influence the more basic human nature of the guest.

A group of researchers at Arizona State University explored the power of social norms in influencing guests to reuse their towels. In one study, a group of 260 guests were randomly assigned one of five cards that explained how reusing towels would conserve energy and save the environment. The messages included:

- "Help the hotel save energy," focusing on the benefit to the hotel.

- "Help save the environment," emphasizing environmental protection.

- "Partner with us to help save the environment," centering on environmental cooperation.

- "Help save resources for future generations," highlighting the benefit to future generations.

- "Join your fellow citizens in helping to save the environment."

The most successful message was the last one — the descriptive norm. A total of 41% of these guests reused their towels. Researchers found the least effective message was the one that emphasized the benefit to the hotel leading to only 20% of guests reusing their towels.[19]

Basically, the research shows what we already know — that we all want to feel that we're normal. Guests want to fit in with the other guests staying at the hotel. If they were told that most of the other guests were reusing their towels, they would probably follow their lead. This is the standard mental response to dealing with something that doesn't fit one's existing worldview — do what we already know works, or follow the crowd because there isn't any reason to think they are wrong.

The challenge we all face — in terms of shifting behaviors, but also with regard to spurring people to use and apply their imagination — is to overcome their resistance. There are many reasons they might resist, and most people are not even conscious of what drives their decisions. People are not protesting or fighting for their rights to keep the status quo in order. They just don't know what the future holds, so it is easier to keep on track with what is already happening. As my chemistry teacher liked to say "It's easier to sit on the couch than it is to go running."

The resistance — or what might be better described as an inertia problem — can be heightened in many different ways. In the case of the towels, the prompt provided by the hotel pre-sents us with a choice to make. Our imagination either becomes active, and we consider the long-term benefits of reusing that one towel on the earth as a whole, even though we can't fully comprehend them, or it doesn't and we don't think twice before allowing the towel to drop to the floor. But remember, our imag-ination is always on and active. Whether or not our imagination gets our attention can be influenced by what else is happening around us, and what we believe and how we perceive our role in relation to the environment as a whole. Our imagination may be focusing on the big issues, while we are more concerned with something more basic — like whether we prefer a clean towel regardless of the environmental impact.

Scientific studies have shown that the imagination can be suppressed when stress levels are elevated — whether that results from ongoing pressure at work, or as a day-to-day reality for communities that are constantly subject to violence, economic inequality, and other issues. Any form of trauma will result in people being less motivated to use their imagination or to take action to improve their situation. The very element of possibility that imagination presents can provide the inspiration to fuel political change and forward progress, in the optimal conditions.

In any political campaign, some voters will view the current state of affairs in a positive light while others will have a different perspective based on their perception of the experience. No matter how well presented or reasoned an argument may be, someone who is already frustrated with the state of affairs of the nation will struggle to believe that change is possible. Failed attempts at persuasion will make the success of future attempts more difficult because resistance can be self-reinforcing.

People don't often recognize the role of imagination in politics — but sharing a vision and detailing a path to a better future exactly how politicians break through — A chicken in every pot; A bridge to the 21st century; Yes We Can; Make America Great Again. Whatever the slogan or tagline is offered by the candidate, when a politician is able to inspire a voter with their ideas or words, they will find success. Of course, a candidate's ideas and words can inspire voters in negative ways as well, by encouraging actions that foment anger or encourage violence. Either way, we gravitate visionary leaders because they trigger our imagination and help us envision the prospect of a future that is better than what is happening now.

The same is true with social change efforts. While people will almost certainly acknowledge that inequalities exist, and believe they should not, their understanding of how to take control and change the situation is often limited. We struggle to imagine a world that is different than the one in which we are living, and thus don't know how to go about realizing a different future. The actions that end up being taken, absent imagination, don't ultimately drive the desired change. People tend to become frustrated or resigned to their current reality — all of which further limits the use of imagination. It's a vicious cycle.

In 2016, in a commencement address at Loyola Marymount University, former President Bill Clinton told graduates that they were fortunate to be alive during the most interdependent age in human history. Their lives, he explained, would always be impacted by what happens to other people, and "by how you react to it, how they treat you, how you treat them, and what larger forces are at work in the world." He acknowledged that there has been an explosion of economic, social, and political empowerment over the past few years, and that it has helped bring issues of race, inequality, and political and social instability to the forefront. But he also cautioned that while it might be tempting to let anger or violence shape people's perceptions and actions, new and different options need to be considered. He told the graduates, "Set the world on fire with your imagination, not with your matches."[20]

Words and images can make us feel we are a part of something, or believe something is true (or the opposite). Whether it takes the form of marketing, news coverage, advocacy, or political rhetoric, how we frame and discuss issues will play a big role in shaping what we think and how we act. Our imagination helps to inform how we view the world, and provides us with the opportunity to create a new world that better suits our needs.

Rational Actors Are Still Just Actors

In the fields of economics and political science, conventional wisdom has long held that people generally will act in ways that support their fundamental views and preferences. For example, while few observers would be surprised if a lifelong Democrat cast a vote for a Democratic candidate in a presidential election, but they might not expect a Republican to go against his or her own party affiliation and vote for a Democratic candidate.

The idea behind the "rational actor" theory — that people seek to act in their own self-interest — sounds perfectly logical. But it fails to explain what causes some voters to change their political views or preferences over time. A group of political scientists at Harvard and Stanford universities, drawing from longstanding social psychology research, have concluded that a person's political attitudes are actually a consequence of the actions he or she has taken — not a cause. According to a working paper they published, changing political attitudes can be understood in the context of "cognitive dissonance," a theory of behavioral psychology that asserts that people experience uneasiness after acting in a way that appears to conflict with their beliefs and preferences about themselves or others. To minimize that mental discomfort, the theory posits, a person will adapt their attitude to better fit with or justify previous actions.

The research also suggests that if political parties can get young people to vote for their candidates at an early age, that could "lock in benefits" over the long term. "What we know is that just the act of voting for a candidate seems to increase your affiliation toward that political party over time and makes you a more habitual voter over time."[21] This is another example of the inertia challenge discussed above, where someone who is on track to think and act a certain way is much more likely to keep on that same track.

The same challenge is faced by every political candidate, in every race they run — and even more so for new candidates or challengers trying to unseat an incumbent. "As candidate you don't need to take the old debates. You can create new ones and reframe things. That's why campaigns are so interesting." Jake Siewert explained. "I started working with Bill Clinton in 1991. And people didn't give him much of a chance because they just didn't ... they were looking at the facts on the ground as they were that day. President Bush was still extremely popular.

Nobody realized the extent of his vulnerability if Clinton were able to shift the tone of the debate away from his glorious victory in Iraq to more domestic concerns." Of course, we all know how that one turned out.

Ideas have power. So do the words and images that are used to introduce and communicate an idea. We must be careful about what we say and how we respond when people use their imagination, so that we can encourage people to think bigger and try new things. Without that use of imagination, we won't be ready for whatever comes next — in business, government, the arts, education, or any other sector. But using our imagination we can see the future we want and work to make it happen.

Challenge: What Are Your Biggest Problems?

We all have problems. Whether you realize it or not, many others face the same, or similar, challenges in their lives. Answering this question will encourage you to imagine how your problems relate to others, and think about how addressing your problems might also lead to solutions that benefit others. When we truly take a step back and start to figure out where are we spending the most time, what would we like to be different, what are the aspects of our life we feel that could get easier, that's when imagination really starts to happen.

To Do: Answer the question: What are the biggest problems that you deal with in your life that you would like to address? Not the little annoyances or the disappointment that results from missed opportunities — what is truly problematic in your life that you would like to stop?

Challenge: Be a "Yes, And ..." Person

One of the basic tenets of improv comedy is known as "Yes, and ...." No matter what your fellow actors present to you, instead of negating it, belittling it, or disagreeing with it, your job is to say, "Yes, and ...." You must accept the scenario as it's presented to you (regardless of where you wanted it to go), and then to add to it.

> *To Do*: Commit to responding "Yes, And ..." to every request, conversation, and situation you encounter — at work, at school, at home, wherever — for one day. See what happens.

NOTES

1. https://www.sciencedaily.com/releases/2015/11/151119104105.htm
2. https://www.sciencedaily.com/releases/2015/11/151119104105.htm
3. http://trendwatching.com/trends/10trends2010/
4. Interview with Jake Siewert — July 29, 2015.
5. https://hbr.org/2013/05/what-a-good-moonshot-is-really-2/
6. http://www.wired.com/2013/02/moonshots-matter-heres-how-to-make-them-happen/
7. http://www.wired.com/2013/01/ff-qa-larry-page/
8. http://www.wired.com/2013/02/moonshots-matter-heres-how-to-make-them-happen/
9. http://www.nytimes.com/aponline/2016/07/28/business/ap-us-alphabet-moonshots.html?_r=0
10. Interview with Marty Neumeier — October 25, 2015.
11. Interview with Bradley Feinstein — July 29, 2015.
12. Interview with Bryan Johnson — August 19, 2015.
13. https://en.wikipedia.org/wiki/Roger_Bannister
14. Interview with Sree Sreenivasan — August 17, 2015.
15. https://www.weforum.org/agenda/2016/06/the-poetry-of-progress
16. *Ansel Adams. An Autobiography* — February 1, 1996.
17. Interview with Jamie Rose — September 14, 2015.
18. Interview with Sarah Stiles — October 20, 2015.
19. Tracey, M.D. (2005). Crafting persuasive pro-environment messages: Psychologists draw from social psychology research to encourage more environmentally friendly behaviors, *Monitor*, *36*(9), http://www.apa.org/monitor/oct05/persuasive.aspx

20. Transcript of President Bill Clinton Commencement at Loyola Marymount University — May 7, 2016, http://lmu.edu/ archives/commencement2016/videosandspeeches/president-billclintonsaddressto2016lmuundergraduates/presidentclinton addressestheundergraduateclassof2016/
21. https://research.hks.harvard.edu/publications/workingpa-pers/citation.aspx?PubId=9751&type=WPN

Imagination and Decision-Making (Information, Experiences, Stuff)

Our perceptions of the world are shaped, and our decisions and actions are informed and motivated by the information we receive and the experiences we have. This chapter demonstrates how using and applying imagination changes how we learn and explore experiences.

It has always been human nature to listen to our friends, our family, and people who we trust when deciding how to spend our time, money, and energy. Over the past couple of decades, with the rise of the Internet and the ubiquity of technology, our relationships and decision-making processes have changed. Audiences do not rely on a single source for information. We don't get our news from one place, all read the same books and magazines, watch the same television shows day after day, or even download and use the same apps. We have incredibly high expectations on everyone and everything: retail, nonprofit organizations and charities, politics and government, media, and education, and our friends and family, whether we engage with them online or offline. Image is (almost) everything.

We each have our preferred networks and communities, people we listen to, and ways of getting information. Technology gives each of us the opportunity to create our own personal connection to something, online and offline. We can essentially get everything we want, customized to meet our personal needs or satisfy our particular interests, have it available on demand or delivered in near-real time, all in return for a price we want to pay, which is often very little. If that thing we want to buy isn't available, we can make our own.

Today, content comes from both institutions and individuals, and audiences recognize the opportunity to learn from a variety of sources and to create and share their own content, to be part of the story. Rather than sit around, they go looking for that information, wherever it is offered. In fact, almost all the growth in the production and distribution of content is in non-institutions — meaning people like us, armed with a device and an idea. Everyone faces the same challenge of competing for attention with anything and everything that is available, as well as becoming a trusted source that people seek out among all the noise.

Our tendency is to look to technology to meet the needs of our audiences. But we must do more than simply log on or build out if we want to have an impact on how people learn and what actions they take. Technology is evolving, audiences continue to shift and the implications of all these massive changes are just beginning to be felt and understood. Technology can be a critical tool in understanding and managing what we do going forward. But technology is just the facilitator of whatever actions are needed. We all have to do more to recognize how quickly everything is changing and what that means to our work.

How people use technology is more important than what the technology itself provides. You couldn't communicate like we do today without technology, but technology wouldn't have much purpose if we didn't want to communicate.

And that's where imagination comes into play.

How Decisions Really Get Made

Why do people buy one product over another? Why do we think someone is trustworthy or not? Why does something that seemed likely to occur just a few days or weeks ago not even considered possible now? Why was someone willing to take a certain action before, but won't now — with no evidence to suggest that they learned, experienced, or tried anything in the interim that would have shifted their perspective or behavior? There are an endless number of questions to ask. We spend a lot of time talking about, and trying to understand, people's behaviors. Entire industries are built on these types of questions.

The research that is conducted and the insights that are shared — about people's buying habits and media consumption, how they spend their time or who they associate with, about people's likes and dislikes, are flawed, or at best, incomplete. We measure what can be quantified. We can measure all sorts of activities and behaviors. We can look at physical and emotional responses to certain situations. But we never know for sure what causes them to occur. There isn't much attention paid to the motivations behind the behaviors, or assessment of what information we need that hasn't yet been measured. We aren't aware of the reasoning behind someone having taken a certain action or think a certain way. In short, nobody asks why.

Ron Klain, Chief Counsel for Revolution Inc (he also served as the United States' Ebola response coordinator), told me that, "Part of the challenge is the multiplicity of scenarios." We were talking about disaster preparedness and what he learned while organizing the global response to the Ebola outbreak in 2015. In our conversation (which was published in an eBook entitled *The Disaster Dialogues*[1]), I suggested that each of our individual networks is fairly easy to map. We have the ability to see who has influence over someone else, under different circumstances, and tailor our approach as a result. He responded:

> Right. But who are the influencers in those situations?
> What messages resonate with us in these times of

crisis — who we're listening to, what we're listening to — that's a hard thing to map in advance of the crisis. Who your influencers are may not be your influencers at times of crisis. So then you may gravitate towards irrational, mistaken, or misguided voices .... Disasters are times when you can change people for the good. There are also times when evil people can exploit people for the bad.

He also noted that people's behaviors, and how they are influenced, change dramatically depending on the situation.

We are invested very heavily in top-down communication from mass media and it almost always fails. "In today's media culture there are no truly trusted authority figures. And so the one-to-many communications through that medium just raises anxiety, doubt, people looking for excuses. I think that the idea that you're going to communicate with people effectively through traditional mass media always fails. So what's the alternative? The alternative is this idea that we've got to get into people's influence networks more directly and have some kind of iterative or interactive communication with people."

That is no easy task, because when the situation changes, so do people's motivations, and the ways that they might be influenced. "I think we classically believe that in the event of fear we defer to authority. What we actually find is when something big happens people start to negate authority. The whole premise of preparation is based on the idea that people are rational, but they aren't. What sort of communication cuts through that?"

In general, we rely way to heavily on individual motivation when it comes to driving action. Getting more people to change their behavior, or take on a task such as disaster preparedness where the potential impact is hypothetical, requires more than just communication. People must be able to imagine the consequences of not preparing, or appreciate the positive benefits of an action they are going to take, without evidence to back it up.

Do Good Intentions Lead to Bad Decisions?

In 2010, a devastating earthquake struck Haiti, killing thousands of people and destroying much of the infrastructure of the already poverty-stricken country. The response to the humanitarian crisis was swift, and at the time, appeared to be unlike anything we had seen before. The amount of money donated, in all forms, to support relief efforts, set records. More importantly, how governments responded, how individuals organized, how technology was used, how the media covered the story — all seemed different than before. The general public's level of interest was greater, compared to previous disasters. Why?

Why were people willing to donate $10 via text message to support earthquake victims in Haiti, but didn't in the wake of the earthquake in the Sichuan Province of China in 2008? The same technology was available, but the idea never caught on.

Why were people willing to collect blankets to be sent to Haiti, but refused to provide the same support to a person living on the street just a few blocks from their home?

Why were companies donating millions of dollars in response to the crisis in Haiti, in some cases far exceeding what they have donated to other causes over the course of a year?

Why did most of the major media choose to fly its top anchors and talent to Haiti, but don't (or won't) send them to Iraq or Afghanistan to report on new developments in those ongoing conflicts?

Why are there dozens of nonprofit organizations competing for attention, and fundraising support, instead of collaborating and coordinating their efforts for greater impact?

Why does the story of the earthquake in Haiti dominate our airwaves, when other, critically important events, including disasters that occur every day don't break through?

There are no doubt plenty of reasonable answers to these questions. There could be political considerations, or logistical challenges that made the response to disasters in the past different. Perhaps, the level of attention paid to this disaster by the media set up the challenge differently so that it reached more people and compelled them to take action. But, do any of those answers really explain why certain decisions were made, or actions were taken?

Many of these considerations get dismissed because an event of this kind gets categorized as an emergency — and is seen as a special case. Do we have any greater understanding now that will help us to learn from this situation and prepare for disasters in the future? Has anyone ever asked why, and pushed until a plausible answer was provided? What if the answer wasn't something that people wanted to hear — a company gave money because it thought it would get them good PR, or a person donated to support earthquake victims in Haiti and not China because they have a bias against China? Have we ever followed up to really determine if the reasons were acceptable or appropriate?

Part of what imagination offers us is the ability to shape our perspective through the narrative surrounding a situation. The facts, the reality of what happened in Haiti, are largely beyond the reach of what Americans can really appreciate. Our experience is not the same, and never will be. At the same time, we are all capable of picturing the bottle of water we helped to fund being delivered to a person in need. Just the same, we can use our imagination to prepare ourselves for the possibility of a disaster, considering different scenarios and what we might need to do to respond. But that doesn't happen enough, because we have an imagination gap, and unless we put our imagination to work beyond that basic — and very limited — reality that we experience every day, we won't ever ask the questions or explore new options further.

Curiosity May Have Killed the Cat — But It Keeps Everyone Else Alive

Megan Smith has overcome quite a few barriers in her life. She is an MIT-trained mechanical engineer and a former vice president in the leadership team of Google X. She was appointed U.S. Chief Technology Officer (CTO) by President Obama in September 2014 and in her role as CTO in the Office of Science and Technology, she helps to shape technology policy, data, and innovation in the United States. She is also a married gay woman in a heavily male-dominated field, working under a microscope in the most power-ful office in the world.

When asked what drives her success, Smith says "intellectual curiosity."

In an interview with Vint Cerf, who is considered as the inventor of the Internet, Smith talked about the importance of being curious. She said, "You're going to live to 100-something years probably if you're born or young today. So you'll have a lot of chances to do a lot of things, so don't pigeonhole yourself. Try a lot of things, and then as you try them, let your passion steer you. You have to find what you want to bring to this world. The more you can be doing the things you love, develop-ing your wonder and curiosity, and being in service to other people, the more you can be helping other people, the more you get back in life."[2]

Curious people are driven by their interest in learning and experiencing new things, more than anything else. As the pace of change in our society continues to accelerate, being curious keeps people happy and motivated, as well as helps to prepare us for whatever might come next. Seeking out new information and ask-ing questions are ultimately a personal endeavor — what makes one of us curious will not be the same as someone else. But no matter the subject area, we will find ourselves sourcing new insights and information from others. We are all part of one, global community — we are all connected. That has always been true in some respects, but thanks to the ready access to media and technology the relative ease with which we can travel the globe, and other modern conveniences, we are also now connected in very practical ways. Our ability to satisfy our own individual curi-osity is greater than ever before.

Our reliance on others, and the influence each of us ultimately can wield, has also grown. This creates the need to understand how others use their imagination. John Seely Brown, the self-titled Chief of Confusion (his more formal title is visiting scholar at USC and the independent cochairman of the Deloitte Center for the Edge), talks about the connection between curiosity and imagination, and how we must go beyond just asking questions to really think about new things. He told an audience at the MacArthur Foundation why he believes we should be focused on imagination:

> The real key is being able to imagine a new world. Once I imagine something new, then answering how to get from here to there involves steps of creativity. So I can be creative in solving today's problems, but if I can't imagine something new, then I'm stuck in the current situation ...

> Art enables us to see the world in different ways. I'm riveted by how Picasso saw the world. How does being able to imagine and see things differently work hand-in-hand? Art education, and probably music too, are more important than most things we teach. Being great at math is not that critical for science, but being great at imagination and curiosity is critical.[3]

Seely Brown's work is focused on changing and improving educational systems. His beliefs about how we learn apply equally to adults as well as to young people. In an interview he explained how the process of learning in the 21st century is changing:

> Traditionally, a person who can answer a given question is said to *know* the answer. We say that person has explicit knowledge. It is content that is easily identified, articulated, transferred, and testable. In general, explicit knowledge is what the educational system teaches. But, it's not the only kind of knowledge there is.

> The twenty-first century, however, belongs to the tacit. In the digital world, we learn by doing, watching, and experiencing. Generally, people don't take a class or read books or manuals to learn how to use a Web browser or e-mail program. They just start doing it,

learning by absorption and making tacit connections. And the more they do it, the more they learn. They make connections between and among things that seem familiar. They experiment with what they already know how to do and modify it to meet new challenges or contests. In a world where things are constantly changing, focusing exclusively on the explicit dimension is no longer a viable model for education.[4]

Our learning systems are still explicit. The same is true for how we approach business and most sectors of our economy today. Our appetite for true experimentation and risk-taking is limited. Even though many have embraced the idea of innovation, they don't realize that the small, constant, incremental improvements in what we know and can do, while measureable and useful, are not the same as the ambitious, novel ideas that our imagination can surface.

We approach innovation through the lens of analysis and interpretation, essentially turning it into a process focused on rational decision-making and problem solving. That approach works well when you are looking for a solution to a relatively well-defined problem. But we are not always trying to solve a problem, sometimes we need to be looking for a new insight, and that means welcoming in different inputs and ideas wherever possible. If we read or watch the same things, we will not gain different perspectives on issues. If we always travel the same route, the chances that we will see or experience something new will be diminished. Just as new innovative ideas are more likely to occur when people and organizations with different backgrounds and perspectives come together, the diverse ways that you try to satisfy your curiosity will result in even more fuel for your imagination.

Learning and working has always required us to go beyond today's problems, methods, and tools. We need to keep looking for new problems to solve as well as for novel approaches to existing problems. Doing so effectively requires an open mind, curiosity, and imagination. We need to be more curious in order to give our imagination the greatest opportunity to flourish.

Do Really, Really Hard Things

Doing new things is hard — really hard. To do something new once, let alone to be able to constantly come up with new and compelling ideas, assumes that a number of important ingredients are all in place. You have to be smart, and engaged, and connected, and have enough free time to really focus — and not always be forced in to a position where you have problems to solve, deadlines to meet, and so on. You probably need some luck, not to mention the support and participation of others (or at least no active opposition). Do you have that kind of freedom in your day? Do you have the ability to commit to driving innovation, with everything else that is required of you in your life?

And beyond that, innovation doesn't just happen. You don't see something on your walk to work in the morning and then translate that into a radical change in your business model, or develop an entirely new set of products before lunch. Sometimes people don't have the time to focus on what needs to change. Maybe they don't have the access to information or the tools they need to explain or demonstrate what changes are needed. In many cases, the changes that occur happen over years or even generations, and without the benefit of a crystal ball, you can't be sure the short-term actions will have the desired impact over time.

None of those are intended as judgments on the intelligence or commitment of the people in the world today who are trying to drive change. All the talk about innovation is not resulting in the kinds of progress that we truly need. Expanding the conversation and the work to include imagination gives us the opportunity to shape our future around new ideas and opportunities. But we cannot escape the conversation about innovation — not to mention ignore the value of continually making improvements and changes. What should we be doing? Let's start by thinking differently about the challenges we face, and committing to doing the really difficult things.

Redefine innovation. Innovation is about incremental shifts in behavior, attitude, and action. Innovation results in measurable improvements to what we already know and how we function today. You don't have to radically change a whole community or measure a huge impact to have done some good. One tiny shift in how someone goes about his or her day that you helped to drive could be a sign of innovation. One change in the way an organization operates is a sign of innovation.

Focus innovation where it can have the greatest impact. The word innovation is used for any effort to drive change, and misapplied when used to describe the creation or transformation of entire industries or parts of our society. We all have the potential to be innovative, if we look at the everyday, ordinary, mundane things in our lives and consider how they might be improved or changed. When we're talking about massive change, innovation is not the priority or the best word to use.

Knowing Is Only Half the Battle

Children of the 1980s may remember the TV cartoon *G.I. Joe*, which told the saga of a fearless, globe-trotting special missions force that works to combat Cobra, an organization with an evil commander bent on world domination. On land, on sea, and in the air — whenever trouble breaks out around the world, *G.I. Joe* is there, ready to battle for ideals that America values. Each episode ended with the good guys having won, the moral of the story made clear, and the show's famous tagline: "Now you know. And knowing is half the battle."

In previous chapters, we discussed the role that knowledge plays in helping to close the imagination gap. Knowledge feeds our imagination — as well as validates the choices that we make. But there is plenty of evidence to show that simply knowing will not result in a true change in behavior or an action being taken. We also need leadership.

Take healthy eating as one example. America has an obesity epidemic with as many as two-thirds of Americans overweight. Various efforts have been made to inform and encourage citizens to change their habits — one such effort in New York included a requirement that restaurants post the calorie counts of meals on their menus. Policy makers continue to believe that the problem is people's lack of knowledge that they are wolfing down calorie-rich foods. But people don't understand what calories really mean, nor do they make the connection between eating and exercising. It is assumed that once Americans know what they are eating, they would eat less, or at least with health in mind. It isn't working.

In contrast, in January 2011, Wal-Mart announced a new program to promote more healthful foods. Wal-Mart is the biggest grocer in the country — serving more than 140 million consumers each week, so their announcement — which included a pledge to reduce sodium by 25% and sugars by 10% in thousands of packaged foods they offer — as a part of their private label brand, Great Values — helped to accelerate the work toward to fight childhood obesity and diabetes across the United States. Because it works with and distributes products from more than 60,000 suppliers, one move by Wal-Mart had a direct impact on hundreds of other companies, whose recipes, production plans, and other business processes needed to be adapted.

Wal-Mart could have used their reach and influence over customers to encourage healthier eating. But that wasn't going to work — for the same reasons that publishing calorie counts on menus alone does not compel someone eating in a restaurant or standing at the counter in a Dunkin Donuts to make smarter choices about their eating. The company could also have asked its customers for input to help shape their strategy and decisions on these issues, but that would assume the customers know what they need, or what's in their best interests, and there is evidence to suggest that customers don't understand these issues.

Instead, Wal-Mart understood that it needed to create an environment where change would just happen. We all need to create an optimal environment for change, individually, as well as, within the organizations we are a part of, at work or on a personal level. We need to create conditions where new ideas can thrive, become contagious, and get executed well. Closing the imagination gap and allowing the new, ambitious possibilities to be explored won't happen without real commitment.

We cannot force people to think up new, big, exciting things. You can't dictate how people view the world, or what information they use to feed their imagination. Too much structure has a chilling effect on people using their imagination. But there are some steps that can be taken.

Provide guidance. Help people to recognize the value or their imagination and appreciate the ways in which their ideas can be captured, shared, and organized. Point people in a general direction, encourage them to be curious and explore whatever comes to mind, and then capture every idea and find ways to explore all of them.

Seek out and invite participants. Some people believe they have an active imagination and others will never raise their hand to offer a new thought, believing that the value of what their imagination generates pales in comparison to others. Don't let only those who opt-in to dominate the conversation. Make sure that you encourage everyone to use their imagination (especially people who have convinced themselves they don't have any ideas to offer); draft them if you have to.

Keep pushing. Demand more ideas. Never be satisfied that an idea has been fully explored or that all the potential options have been exhausted. It is far too common for organizations to take whatever whiff of innovation they might uncover and run with it — instead of expanding their search and allowing their imagination to flourish.

Try stuff. Instead of pursuing projects, or picking up on the first idea that comes out and trying to run with it, try lots of different things. Support whatever it takes to make new things happen, to learn differently, to gain knowledge in ways and from places that are not part of the normal patterns.

To break out of the old habits and patterns, we need a whole new way of doing things. We will need a whole new team. But let me be clear: that doesn't mean it is necessary to get rid of an existing team in favor of new staff (or volunteers, or board members, or partners). It doesn't mean go out and hire someone who has an active imagination. We all have imaginations. We need to make it possible for the people who are part of our organization, who we work alongside every day, to change their thinking, to use and apply their imagination. We need to adapt our operation so that your team can put their imaginations to work in the best ways.

A good place to start is by making people uncomfortable.

Be Uncomfortable

When building a culture to encourage and support innovation, one of the most important rules cited is the need to create a safe space. Anyone who has ever been in a classroom or company meeting knows the potential risk of saying something outlandish — only to invite a rebuke from the teacher or boss, or at the very least attract awkward glances from classmates and colleagues. The idea or thought might be dismissed as silly, frivolous, ignorant, leaving the person who suggested it feeling alienated and embarrassed for speaking up. Without a sense of safety, most people will decide to silence an unconventional statement that could risk their standing.

A safe space offers stability and protection from the challenges that we face in real life. But safe spaces, in protecting us against the noise and criticism that exist all around us, have a chilling effect on the use of our imagination. Safety blocks out what we need to learn and experience to feed our imagination. To push our imagination to the fullest, we need to be uncomfortable.

In recent years, as political rhetoric has escalated, discussions about race and inequality have found their way into public discourse, college students across the country have complained that they no longer feel safe and welcome. The idea of "safe spaces" on campuses emerged to help maintain civility and foster constructive discussion. But these safe spaces have also had another, unintended effect, of shutting off debate.

In his Commencement address to the University of Michigan in 2016, tech-billionaire and former NYC Mayor, Michael Bloomberg, challenged the idea of safe spaces:

> The most useful knowledge that you leave here with today has nothing to do with your major. It's about how to study, cooperate, listen carefully, think critically and resolve conflicts through reason. Those are the most important skills in the working world, and it's why colleges have always exposed students to challenging and uncomfortable ideas.

> The fact that some university boards and administrations now bow to pressure and shield students from these ideas through "safe spaces," "code words" and "trigger warnings" is, in my view, a terrible mistake.

> The whole purpose of college is to learn how to deal with difficult situations — not run away from them. A micro-aggression is exactly that: micro. And one of the most dangerous places on a college campus is a safe space, because it creates the false impression that we can insulate ourselves from those who hold different views.

> We can't do this, and we shouldn't try — not in politics or in the workplace. In the global economy, and in a democratic society, an open mind is the most valuable asset you can possess.[5]

Everyone deserves to be safe — not to fear violence or persecution because of what they believe or the ideas they have. Everyone should be able to speak up and share their views, whether that is on a college campus, in a brainstorm at work, or wherever. But the idea of safe spaces in practice has had the effect of preserving existing ideas and ways of thinking as well. Our capacity to use our imagination and to consider what isn't possible yet requires access to the maximum diversity of experiences, perspectives, and considerations. It benefits from some tension and cross-pollination of ideas that wouldn't otherwise be encouraged to mix. Safe spaces have limited our access to new information and experiences. But our imagination benefits when we are made to feel a little uncomfortable.

Imagination is about seeing the impossible, or unreal. With imagination, our focus can be on things that are impossible, not just what is right in front of us or consumes us in the here and now. It's important to know the differences, and to know when you're using one mode of thinking as opposed to the other, and what the context is for that reasoning.

There are lots of ways to feed our imagination. Everything we do contributes to our imagination, which is why it is so important to make an effort to maximize the diversity of your inputs. We can read books or blogs that align with our interests because it helps to enhance your knowledge. But it is equally important that we also consume information that we disagree with or find boring. Travel can open our minds to new cultures, but be careful not to visit the same places over and over. Tasting a new type of food or browsing a new store in your neighborhood helps to build knowledge and feed our imagination, but don't frequent the same new places over and over, or the impact is diminished.

The best way to approach the challenge of continually feeding our imagination is to think like a kid again — and to pursue new inputs and knowledge with a full sense of wonder and openness. People are going to suggest ideas and attempt things that have already been done — and that is part of the learning process. But if you create a safe space where the experiences and perspectives of a connected society are not integrated, you limit what will be created. We need to come up with endless ideas and endless concepts. We have to just commit to keep going until we create them.

Challenge: Three People, Three Perspectives

Make up three different characters (three people that are nothing like you). Give them names, occupations, and try to make a rough mental picture of how they look — remember that the less like you the better. Spend a couple of minutes thinking about the details of these people's fictional lives. Give them personalities and a few habits. Base them on someone you know, or just pull the characters out of the air if that is easier. Get to know them because they are going to help you solve a lot of problems in the future. Simply because you are attempting to answer the question on behalf of someone very different from you, you will come up with some remarkable solutions. No matter what situation you put [Person X] in, you will come up with solutions that would not naturally occur in your thoughts.

To Do: Imagine how another person would behave in your situation. Pose your problem to each of your characters in turn. Quickly write down 10 responses from each: "What would [Person X] do in this situation?"

Challenge: Who Can You Learn Something From?

Every time you learn something new, your brain changes in a pretty substantial way. In turn, this makes other parts of your life easier because the benefits of learning stretch further than just being good at something. Learning a new skill has all kinds of unexpected benefits, including improving working memory, better verbal intelligence, and increased language skills. Of course, seeking out and mastering something new on your own can be a daunting task. But you can always ask for help.

To Do: Think about who you know, or want to know, that could teach you something. Anything. Then ask that person for help learning something new. It could be a small thing, or a whole new profession. You could learn something from one-time conversation or set up a recurring lesson. But it has to start with someone else.

NOTES

1. *The Disaster Dialogues* — Edited by Brian Reich. http://www. littlemmedia.com/disaster-dialogues/ (pp. 21–27).
2. http://cacm.acm.org/magazines/2015/6/187315-an-interview-with-us-chief-technology-officer-megan-smith/fulltext
3. http://spotlight.macfound.org/featured-stories/entry/john-seely-brown-beyond-creativity-cultivate-imagination/
4. http://www.thedailyriff.com/articles/conversations-with-john-seely-brown-1062.php
5. https://www.bloomberg.com/view/articles/2016-04-30/here-s-your-degree-now-go-defeat-demagogues

Imagination and Expectation (Beliefs and Behaviors)

There are established cultural beliefs and ingrained behaviors that we accept as the norm. Their very existence limits our ability to engage and motivate people to take any sort of action. This chapter outlines how using and applying imagination can change beliefs and behaviors, and expand our individual and collective potential.

Imagination plays a big role in what we believe and how we see the world that we cannot explore directly through experience. We don't touch, or smell, or see our faith — it is inside us. Moreover, regardless of whether you actively practice a religion or not, believe there is anthropological evidence to support the stories found in the *Bible, Quran, Torah*, and other religious literature or not — you cannot deny that imagination is a key part of faith.

What can we understand about religion by thinking about faith? Plenty.

Jew-ish

A 2013 study from the Pew Research Center's Religion and Public Life Project found that 20% of American Jews classify themselves as "of no religion" and that 58% of American Jews have intermarried.[1] The Pew study describes these people as "cultural" Jews. I am a cultural Jew.

I dropped out of Sunday School when I was in fourth grade, but thanks to help from a tutor, I was Bar Mitzvah'd at the age of 13. I know the customs and traditions of the Jewish faith. I proudly identify as a member of "the tribe." I have certainly enjoyed my fair share of challah and noodle kugel through the years. But, aside from dropping in on an occasional High Holiday service or funeral, you won't find me spending much time in a synagogue, lighting Friday night candles or donning a yarmulke.

I have been told over and over again that being a cultural Jew is not Jewish enough. I am judged by people who are more actively involved with organized Judaism and the verdict is that I am Jew-ish (which is not intended as a compliment).

Over the years, I have been asked by a number of different Jewish organizations for help to find ways to encourage "cultural Jews" like myself to become more actively involved. The conversation always starts with someone saying they are looking for new ideas and opportunities, the conversation always ends up in the same place: with someone asking the question "how do we get people to ... (fill in the blank)." How do we get more people to join our youth groups? How do we get more people to sign up for a class? How do we get people to join our synagogue and attend more services?

This line of thinking is pervasive in Jewish life — and most every other type of organization, religious or otherwise, as well. People think the problem is that they haven't done a good enough job marketing their product — be it a membership or the broader worldview that they embrace. What they aren't doing is imagining all the ways that what they are offering — an opportunity to be more involved in Jewish life and culture (however you want to define that) — could be approached differently, so it is interesting to people who are not currently engaged.

Faith and religion are rooted in imagination. There is an opportunity for any of us to imagine our own relationship with a higher power and to shape our connection to faith in whatever ways we find most appropriate. Rick Warren, pastor of the Saddleback

Church, author of the *Purpose Driven Life*, and one of the most well-known religious scholars and advocates in the world believes this. He wrote:

> When you can't see something physically, you have to imagine it in your mind. Imagination is essential to living by faith.
>
> Hebrews 11:1 says, *"Faith is the confidence that what we hope for will actually happen; it gives us assurance about things we cannot see"* (NLT, second edition).
>
> Faith is when we hope for something, and we know it's going to happen. In order to hope for something, you have to picture it in your mind.[2]

Maurice Bloch, a well-known cultural anthropologist, also believes that religion is a product of imagination. Writing in a journal article in 2008, he explained, "Religious-like phenomena in general are an inseparable part of a key adaptation unique to modern humans, and this is the capacity to imagine other worlds, an adaptation that I argue is the very foundation of the sociality of modern human society." He added, "Once we realize this omnipresence of the imaginary in the everyday, nothing special is left to explain concerning religion."[3]

Bloch's point is that imagination is critical to human development. Consider the ability to engage spontaneously in pretend play — something children do at a very young age, and develop further over time. Nothing like that occurs in other species. Imagination, in other words, is part of what makes us unique as humans. Our ability to believe that things we have not yet experienced can be real is what sets us apart.

Isaac Luria is a movement leader, faith-rooted organizer, and social impact technologist who specializes in how the stories we tell shape our lives and change the world. His mother was a minister and an organizer — one of the first women ever trained by Saul Alinsky to be an organizer. His father was a professor and historian of religious progressive movements. "My table talk, my dinner conversation was very much about how could religion be a progressive force in the world. I considered myself spiritual, but not religious,"[4] he told me.

As we talked about the connections between faith and imagination, Luria told me that it's difficult to speak generally about faith because there are so many different ways that people approach it. "For a lot of people, faith is a way to split up their world into categories they can understand — good and evil, good and bad, right and wrong." He added that "Everybody has a fear of imagination. And, in a faith context, what allows faith to go further is that it gives people permission to take a leap, to make a way out of no way. And I think that the unknowing, the humility around unknowing, I think allows a more imaginative approach to take route."

Macky Alston, who organizes trainings to help social justice movement organizers advance their issues, says he uses what he calls a "love-based approach." He says he tries to break down the barriers that individuals impose on themselves that prevent them from believing something is possible. "The love-based approach is really a strengths-based approach — believing people to the point where they have eliminated the sensors, eliminated the self-doubt and unleashed their capacity to imagine. That strategy has worked with the people I have helped to mentor. It is the strategy that is going to work in our education systems. It's going to work for my kids; as I raise my kids I can tell the biggest enemies in their brains are their beliefs that they can't do something or that they're not smart."[5]

Part of what it means to be human is to believe in something and our faith traditions tell us to stand up for what we believe. Meanwhile, we grow up in societies that teach us not to rock the boat. We are rewarded for getting with the program. We are often punished if we rock the boat. We don't need faith traditions, or workplace norms, or standardized tests to determine who we are. That's what we have our imagination for. Once we recognize that we have a radical capacity for imagination, everything else will start to change.

The Problem Is that We're Not Asking the Best Questions

Asking the right questions and making the connections between the day-to-day work that consumes our lives (professionally and personally) and the larger context surrounding an issue is something we all can do better. There are tools and systems that will help you track progress or offer reminders to take certain steps. But the biggest thing people need is "confidence," says Jamie Rose. "If you believe that you can do anything, and you are limitless in your ability to create, then it is very easy to come up with the next thing, the next solution, the next product, the next creative endeavor, or whatever that is. Once you demonstrate that you can do creative stuff, you will be identified or labeled as a creative person and you will go down that path."[6]

A confident person is more likely to accept that when trying out a new experience, mistakes are inevitable, and that if one (or many) should happen, they can handle it. They know that if they give something their best effort, whatever happens will work out fine. Their confidence is rooted in their own ability and capacity to imagine how things could go in the future. With that positive outlook they put themselves in the very best mental state to master that new situation. That's why confidence is so important to imagination.

With confidence in your ability to deal with any situation, or contribute something interesting from your imagination, you are willing to take things on that others might not even consider. Imagination also allows that to happen because you are able to envision a future that is not what you are familiar with. But people's overall confidence, just like imagination, gets slowly eroded over time.

"I have a two year old. Her entire job right now is to have fun. Her entire job is to play and to enjoy herself and to have good ideas. She does not have responsibilities other than going to sleep when we tell her to. So her entire job right now, and her entire life is based on fostering her imagination and growing her imagination,"[7] Peter Shankman told me. But, he continued "At some point as she gets older — and I'm hoping it doesn't happen to her but it happened to us; it probably will — she will be told, not by us, her parents, but by others out there in the world, that having an imagination or letting your imagination dictate too much, is wrong. I hope she doesn't believe that. I don't believe that. I have been successful with that in my life, and I believe the majority of things I have achieved are because I've allowed my imagination to run free."

If you think about anyone who has ever changed the world, in any capacity, it is because they've imagined something different. But very few people are given that opportunity, or put in that kind of environment. "Most people still work at a company where they are told, 'Do it this way because that's the way we've always done it', and imagination is often frowned upon," Shankman suggested. "That's sad; that's very, very sad but that is the nature of where we are and I think we need to fix it."

Consider how we approach problem solving. How could we make it so that everybody used mass transportation? What if we made riding the subway or bus something that everyone could do for free, always? What if we made it illegal or impossible to drive a car? The questions we ask, and how we ask them, dictates how far we will allow our thinking to reach.

"The problem is that we're not asking the best questions,"[8] suggests Kurt Ronn. "Solving a big problem versus a small problem; there's a fallacy in the way we think and we're taught this all the time. If I ask you which one is easier to solve, a big problem or a small problem, most people would say, "Well, of course, a small problem," and they would be wrong. That is a cognitive bias."

Size is most likely the wrong way to think about which challenges can or cannot be solved. It is an equally bad way to measure the quality of an idea. Complexity is the better orientation. If a small problem has been around for a long time, it is almost certainly not easy to solve. It may seem less challenging than something more expansive, and yet it still persists. That is one of the reasons why it is important to make the connections between different issues, and ideas, and appreciate the larger context in which they exist. As Kurt Ronn notes "Being able to stay focused, keep working on something is a skill that you have to learn if you are going to live a meaningful life – but you also have to be looking around. We need to be better at daydreaming. Because your vision is what actually adds meaning in life, and helps shape your mission, so that the things you do, the actual execution, achieves what you want and provides you the positive feedback you need."

Move Fast — Change Everything

On a typical day, my time will be spent roughly as follows:

- Check my email and process it as quickly as possible — delete, file, respond, or similar.
- Open a document to write something.
- Log into Facebook to see what my friends are posting about, and then toggle to a news site or blog to read a well-written or useful article.
- Switch back to the writing.
- Clean up — maybe go through a stack of paper on my desk.
- Back to the writing.
- Text a question to my wife.
- Walk over to the desk of a colleague to share an idea for a project.
- Check email.
- More writing.
- *Repeat.*

Some form of this — where I move quickly between activities, without ever really focusing deeply on any one thing, especially the writing that is makes up the majority of my work responsibilities — is the norm. Most of the time when I am at work I am in "frantic mode." I don't focus deeply on any one thing while I am in frantic mode.

The opposite approach would be "flow mode." Scott Barry Kauffman, the Director of the Imagination Institute, wrote that, "When in flow, the creator and the universe become one, outside distractions recede from consciousness and one's mind is fully open and attuned to the act of creating. There is very little self-awareness or critical self-judgment; just intrinsic joy for the task."[9] He stressed that flow was essential to creativity and well-being in a variety of different parts of our lives, and that research is starting to show that flow is more strongly related to personality than cognitive ability.

Operating in frantic mode has some obvious benefits — I engage in a range of different activities, contribute to a variety of conversations and check a lot of things off my to-do list. My inbox stays manageable. And, each of the activities I engage with provides me with new inputs, thus feeding my imagination and sparking new questions and thoughts that might be useful later. It's like speed dating for information. Admittedly, focusing on writing something longer or more thoughtful can be challenging when constantly shifting focus from one thing to the next. When I switch to flow mode – turn everything off, shut everything out, the words start to pour out.

We are much more connected to devices and supported by technology than ever before. That's not just at work — our phone makes us available at all times, and offers us access to information on demand. Our homes are enabled with "smart" devices — to help regulate the thermostat or make reheating leftovers that much easier. In an increasingly connected world, there are more opportunities to be in frantic mode. It takes real discipline to put yourself into a place where you have the ability to focus on just one task.

The argument against constant switching is that it impacts productivity. That is true. It is generally counterproductive if you're working on one task and you're interrupted on a completely different topic. You have to shift your cognitive resources — or attentional resources in brain scientist speak — to something else.

And when you shift your thinking, it can take you a while to get into a rhythm, not to mention taking you time to get back and remember where you were. You are never fully present in what you are doing.

Generally, the discussion about frantic versus flow mode is oriented around productivity. Clearly you can get more done when in frantic mode, but will be more successful doing things that require thought when in flow mode. Depending on your frame of reference, one will be better than the other. But that line of thinking is too simplistic. In the digital age, we need technology. You cannot survive without the communication and productivity tools. You also need to switch regularly between frantic and flow modes in order to maximize the potential of your brain and unlock the full power of your imagination.

Solving Problems Is About Causing Problems

There has been a lot of research into the psychology of problem solving that says if you let problems incubate, sometimes it helps in discovering a solution. A good example would be a software developer who just can't trace a bug so they put it aside and spend their time on something else. The answer may come to the software developer later while he or she is working on another task or what they end up spending their time will trigger a new thought.

Imagination does not involve a single brain region or single side of the brain. The entire process — from feeding your brain, to having a first spark, to forming a complete idea, to figuring out how to package it for others to understand — consists of many interacting cognitive processes (both conscious and unconscious) and emotions. Depending on where you are in the process, different brain regions are recruited to handle the task. When you call to mind something you've never actually seen, for example, it's a lot easier to think creatively than if you try imagining something that's familiar to you.

Each situation is different. So, really, the best option is not to choose one function over the others, the good stuff happens when you are constantly switching. You want to push your brain to generate ideas sometimes, and then balance that by giving your imagination time to roam. The surest way to provoke the imagination is to seek out environments you have no experience with. If you live in the city, surrounded by noise and businesses, seek out a quiet place in the country every once in a while.

Change Jobs as Often as Necessary

For the first few months after someone is hired at Google they are called Nooglers. There are only a few thousand Nooglers hired each year, from an estimated 2 million applications. What makes someone a good fit at Google? The company website claims "There's no one kind of Googler, so we're always looking for people who can bring new perspectives and life experiences to our teams. If you're looking for a place that values your curiosity, passion, and desire to learn, if you're seeking colleagues who are big thinkers eager to take on fresh challenges as a team, then you're a future Googler."

Google is famous for reengineering the traditional approach to hiring. Their hiring process is calibrated to find applicants who have both intelligence and a capacity for imagination. Laszlo Bock, the Head of People Operations at Google, says the company is interested in people who can solve problems and figure things out when there is no clear answer. Unlike many companies, Google does not consider a high GPA or perfect test scores a good indicator a strong candidate. "Academic environments are artificial environments. People who succeed there are sort of finely trained; they're conditioned to succeed in that environment," he has explained,[10] nor is having a computer science degree a requirement for being hired (even for technical roles).

While Google is a technology company, and they place a high premium on people who have a demonstrated knowledge in computer science, engineering, and other programming related disciplines, they also seek out applicants with "cognitive ability" — what Bock describes as those "who are going to reinvent the way their jobs are going to work rather than somebody who's going to come in and do what everybody else does."[11]

Most companies rely on more traditional measures to identify candidates who are likely to succeed. They review and compare test scores and assume the person who performed better is more qualified. The attributes of the best candidates often don't show up on a resume or academic transcript. When Goldman Sachs analyzed what made certain employees stand out, they found that "people who experience loss or adversity at an early age are apparently much more likely to be successful than people who have been comfortable their whole lives,"[12] Jake Siewert told me. When figuring out who will make the best hire, Siewert explained "You want to get a better sense of that person's life and what drove them and kind of how they got through whatever they got through to come to you. And that's hard. Just having studied this or studied that doesn't really tell you a heck of a lot. I mean I studied renaissance philosophy, and that didn't make me equipped to do anything in particular."

Once a company hires an employee, they generally want them to stay as long as possible, and extract as much value from them over time. That makes sense if you are the one doing the extracting, but not so much if you are the person whose value is being extracted. Today, most people — especially those entering the workforce — aren't thinking about building their careers the way previous generations of workers did. Instead of following some well-worn career path, more and more people are switching jobs regularly to make sure they learn and experience as much as possible throughout their professional endeavors. In a competitive market, they want more, get more, and there is much less risk in switching jobs than ever before.

Changing jobs regularly used to be a flag for hiring managers. Someone who only stayed with an organization for a (relatively) short period of time was thought to be a flawed candidate. Today, job switchers are common, and recognized as ambitious people who are seeking out new challenges and opportunities to learn. According to LinkedIn, professionals who ended up in the Media and Entertainment, Professional

Services, and Government/Education/Nonprofits industries job-hopped the most, while people working in Oil and Energy, Manufacturing/Industrial, and Aero/Auto/Transport industries job-hopped the least.[13] Job hoppers are ambitious, curious employees — looking to do really well at work and to position themselves well for whatever comes next. Even if they are only employed for a limited time, any organization will benefit from having a highly engaged and motivated person on their team.

Switching jobs is one of the best ways to keep your skills sharp and your imagination active and engaged. It takes a good deal of confidence and courage to take on new challenges versus staying somewhere that seems safe. Even if you've found a role that keeps you happy, the world is changing so rapidly that you should constantly be looking for opportunities to learn new skills and do things outside of your comfort zone.

Just because we all have an imagination doesn't mean that it will fire on its own – or that what pops into your head will take shape as something that can be pursued further. Your imagination requires care and feeding. Your imagination needs nourishment. The more you feed your imagination a steady diet of different inputs – maybe a mix of art, music, sports, philosophy, people watching and more – the more your brain will start to fire with ideas. That definitely includes taking on new and different challenges in your work.

Challenge: An Hour a Day

Ben Franklin famously set aside an hour a day to devote to learning. Warren Buffett spends five to six hours per day reading (everything from newspapers to corporate reports), and Bill Gates reads 50 books per year. Mark Zuckerberg committed to running one mile every day, wherever he was in the world, often running — and talking with — a different person each time he laces up his sneakers. Taking time to learn or try something new each day — no matter what you choose to pursue — will arguably be the best investment of time you can make.

To Do: Commit an hour each day to learning, and in doing so, you are feeding your imagination.

NOTES

1. http://www.pewforum.org/2013/10/01/chapter-2-intermarriage-and-other-demographics/
2. http://rickwarren.org/devotional/english/faith-requires-imagination
3. http://rstb.royalsocietypublishing.org/content/royptb/363/1499/2055.full.pdf
4. Interview with Isaac Luria — July 29, 2015.
5. Interview with Macky Alston — July 29, 2015.
6. Interview with Jamie Rose — September 14, 2015.
7. Interview with Peter Shankman — July 29, 2015.
8. Interview with Kurt Ronn — June 15, 2016.
9. http://scottbarrykaufman.com/who-enters-flow/
10. http://www.businessinsider.com/what-google-looks-for-in-employees-2015-4
11. https://www.youtube.com/watch?v=AaXjbwWtRUk
12. Interview with Jake Siewert — July 29, 2015.
13. https://business.linkedin.com/talent-solutions/blog/trends-and-research/2016/job-hopping-has-increased–and-will-accelerate#!

Imagination and Structures (Rules and Standards)

8

The keys to change, for an organization or a society, are motivation and discipline. Within the appropriate structures, and with the necessary rules in place, anything is possible. This chapter outlines how the use and application of imagination influences structures and rules, and foundations on which the future will be built, and better ways to use and apply imagination without undermining what makes our individual imaginations so unique and powerful.

Can You Find Imagination on a Map?

Eric Weiner, a former National Public Radio foreign correspondent turned best-selling author, travels the world in search of different things.

In his book, *The Geography of Bliss*, Weiner went in search of the happiest places and what we can learn from them. He wrote, "I roam the world in search of answers to the pressing questions of our time: What are the essential ingredients for the good life? Why are some places happier than others? How are we shaped by our surroundings?"[1] His travelogue includes places like Iceland (one of the world's happiest countries), Bhutan (where the king has made Gross National Happiness a national priority), Moldova (not a happy place, according to Weiner), and Switzerland (where Weiner discovered the hidden virtues of boredom).

When he visited the Netherlands, he learned about the World Database of Happiness, an archive of research findings (based on a lot of self-reported data from individuals in different countries) on subjective enjoyment of life. The social scientists that Weiner spoke with analyze the data and offer conclusions such as "Wealthy people are happier than poor ones, but only slightly" and "People are least happy when they're commuting to work." Apparently countries that emphasize societal obligations over individual contentment report lower levels of happiness and the world's happiest nations are secular and homogeneous, and often report high suicide rates.

The insight provided by Weiner is compelling for sure, but also incomplete. The data that he reviewed, and the research he conducted through his travels, largely considered historical factors in determining the factors that influence happiness the most. Don't moods change? Can we influence happiness?

The answer appears to be yes. One of the places that Weiner wrote about in his book was Slough (rhymes with cow), a small town outside of London. In 2005, psychologist Richard Stevens initiated an experiment in Slough to determine whether it might be possible to intentionally raise the happiness level of an entire community by promoting certain practices among the population. The experiment was filmed for the BBC and called *Making Slough Happy*.[2]

The basis of the experiment was to test 10 simple measures (the Happiness Manifesto) on a group of volunteers:

1. Plant and nurture something.

2. Count your blessings (at least five/day).

3. Have at least one hour-long conversation with a loved one each week.

4. Phone a friend you've been out of touch with and meet up.

5. Have a tasty treat each day and take plenty of time to enjoy it.

6. Exercise for at least ½ hour at least thrice/week.

7. Smile at and say hello to a stranger at least once a day.

8. Have a good laugh at least once a day.

9. Cut your TV viewing by at least 50%.

10. Do a good deed at least once a day.

There is nothing particularly unique about these directives — countless books and articles on happiness in the self-help section of a bookstore include variations of the same list. What *is* unique about the *Making Slough Happy* experiment is that it is the first (and so far the only) study of a community in which a significant number of participants have consistently engaged in practices over an extended period of time that have produced a measurable increase in happiness levels. Oh, and it worked. Dr. Stevens and his assistants found that there was a 33% increase in the happiness level of the participants in the study. In follow-up studies, they found that the vast majority of the study's participants continued to sustain these increased levels of happiness.

One of the goals of the experiment was to discover what the impact of the results would be on other members of the community who had not participated in the study. The hope was to find that the beneficial effects might also impact the lives of other citizens who did not directly engage in the project. The research did not yield any noticeable improvement on the part of these people, leading researchers to conclude that while each individual does have some influence on his or her experience of happiness, we each have to do our own work in order to reap the results. Put another way, the benefits of individual practices are not contagious — at least not when it comes to happiness.

The *Making Slough Happy* experiment was conducted in a (relatively) static environment, over a limited period of time. Over the course of three months, nothing significant about the population of Slough changed, no major events occurred. By design, the experiment tested the capacity for individuals to change. And it did show that individuals are capable of changing their own happiness. Arguably, almost anything is possible at an individual level. What about at scale?

The *Geography of Bliss* was published in 2007. Do the conclusions that Weiner makes about what factors that contribute to people's happiness still hold up after a decade? As technology has become more prevalent in our society, creating connections between places on opposite sides of the planet that never existed before, are the direct and indirect influences on people's happiness different — or at least should we consider them differently? As more information has become available, and government, corporate and civic leaders have embraced the economic and social benefits of happiness, a lot of money and energy has been invested to try to answer those questions. A lot more is known about how to change individual behaviors — but at scale, most of the same questions still remain.

Large-scale influence on people's behavior is difficult. We are all individuals. Nobody is exactly the same. Dramatically changing an entire population is not easy to do or to test. But what happens when an entire population does change in a relatively short period of time? Consider, for example that a nearly five million people were forced to flee Syria between 2011 and 2016 because of war, terror, and persecution. Over a million refugees flooded into Germany in 2015 alone. These significant shifts in population and the fact that they have been condensed into such a short period of time will influence everything about those countries, including the happiness levels in ways that have never been seen before. Essentially a new laboratory for what Eric Weiner has been exploring has been created, only it's the new reality of the world right now.

In his latest book, titled *The Geography of Genius*, Eric Weiner again hit the road — this time to examine the connection between our surroundings and our most innovative ideas. Weiner visited places that are widely regarded today as beacons of creativity, from the annals of history (Athens) to the more recent past (Silicon Valley). Weiner also found places whose concentrated genius are not as well appreciated, including: Hangzhou, China (which experienced an explosion of culture between the 10th and 13th centuries under the Song dynasty), Edinburgh (where in the 18th-century economists like Adam Smith and David Hume were in residence); Calcutta (where between 1840 and 1920 British culture and Indian culture collided to produce a vibrant intellectual life); and Vienna (which is one of the few, if only, locations that can twice qualify — fostering genius during the era of composers like Mozart and Beethoven and then again in late-19th and early-20th centuries with psychologists like Freud and Klimt).[3]

For Weiner to determine which places deserve credit for fostering genius, he first had to apply some sort of standard to measure against. What exactly *is* genius? Can anyone be a genius — by birth, or through hard work — or genius rooted in someone's capacity to see the world differently, and can only a few people possess those attributes? Does where you live determine whether you are, or will become, a genius?

Immanuel Kant, who coined the term *genius* in the 1700s, defined it as the rare capacity to independently understand concepts that would normally have to be taught by another person. Academics have tried to understand the contributing factors to someone being a genius for centuries, attacking the question from various angles including anthropology, psychology, history, even meteorology. Because so much of that study of genius comes from different discreet areas of study, there are inevitable contradictions. Weiner notes that good weather seems to attract the best and brightest to Silicon Valley — but Vienna and Edinburgh did fine with arguably worse weather. Some studies have suggested a link between sorrow in childhood and individual genius, but there are plenty of examples that suggest that association is neither universal nor predictive.

Many studies — and more pop-sociological assessments, as in the case of Eric Weiner — have looked at concentration of genius, by geography (physical proximity, but also concentration at an academic institution or similar) and whether that contributes. Does having a high concentration of geniuses makes it more likely will attract, or create, more geniuses?

In recent years, believing that you can manufacture genius by squeezing people into a room together, organizations of all types have built dedicated spaces to foster innovation. But this isn't the kind of thing you can cultivate or access on demand. It's not the density of cities, or offices, or anything that makes people capable of using and applying their imaginations in a compelling way. Rather, the way different people and communities interact and form connections factor in to the creation of genius. Open-mindedness — the ability to hold contradictory ideas about the same subject — is a common thread as well.

Research published by scientists from the Massachusetts Institute of Technology (MIT) in 2013 concluded that productivity and innovation in urban areas grow at roughly the same rate as population, largely because the greater density of people living in a city increases the opportunities for personal interactions and exposure to different ideas.[4] The research team analyzed all kinds of factors to calculate the "social-tie density" of different cities or the average number of people each resident will interact with personally. They looked at how many people are sharing a cell tower (literally sharing a signal), the number of people connecting through location-based social networks and the contagion rates of diseases spread only through personal contact. They found that the higher a city's social-tie density, the higher its levels of productivity and greater number of patents awarded.

The model doesn't hold up, however, when you look at the fact that some huge African and Asian cities have even denser populations than cities in the West, and don't generate the same number of patents. The MIT scientists argued the reason is because, generally, those cities have terrible transportation systems — and if people can't get around, they can't have those serendipitous interactions, and thus a city's density has less impact.

But what if the measure of creativity and innovation is not patents, but something else. In his two books, Eric Weiner looked at happiness and "genius." The measure of happiness was self-reported data, and factors in things like longer lifespan or improved productivity. Genius is measured in cultural terms as well as economic impact — which quickly leads to whether an innovation reached a lot of people, earned a patent and similar. What if the best way to measure progress was not through outcomes or outputs, but through change itself? Movement. Progress. Perhaps, societies don't need to be truly happy, just less sad and frustrated than in the past. Maybe hunger doesn't need to be eradicated, but there need to be fewer food-insecure people. For certain, we need to show progress toward some ambitious goal to confirm that we are moving forward at all.

Anything Less Than 100% Isn't Good Enough

The gap that exists for imagination is between what is currently happening and what is possible. There is no limit to imagination. There are no limits to how many new ideas can be offered. Nor, for that matter, are there any limits on how much a company can sell, or how much money a nonprofit can raise, or how many channels exist on your television, and similar. So why do we celebrate those types of measures without consider the larger context of what is possible?

Philanthropic giving in the United States generates about $350 billion annually.[5] But the number of people who give money is relatively small, and pales in comparison to the number of people who spend money on everything else. Is $350 billion a measure of a successful philanthropic sector in the United States? Not when you consider the potential for more Americans to give. Our willingness to measure the success of our philanthropy based on the amount of money raised, and not the application of those dollars or the impact of the investment shows a lack of imagination. Celebrating a growth in fundraising, when the issues that the money raised are supposed to address continue to worse demonstrates that our focus is trained in the wrong places.

Voter turnout in the United States is among the lowest in the developed world. According to Pew:

> Political scientists typically measure turnout by looking at votes cast as a percentage of eligible voters. Since

many hard-to-measure factors can affect eligibility (citizenship, imprisonment, residency rules and other legal barriers), turnout calculations are based on the estimated voting-age population. By that measure, the U.S. lags most of its peers, landing 31st among the 34 countries in the Organization for Economic Cooperation and Development, most of whose members are highly developed, democratic states.

U.S. turnout in 2012 was 53.6%, based on 129.1 million votes cast for president and an estimated voting-age population of just under 241 million people. Among OECD countries, the highest turnout rates were in Belgium (87.2%), Turkey (86.4%) and Sweden (82.6%). Switzerland consistently has the lowest turnout, with just 40% of the voting-age population casting ballots in the 2011 federal legislative elections, the most recent.[6]

Since the end of World War II, voter turnout in the United States has never risen above 65% of the electorate. Only 42% of Americans voted in the 2014 midterm elections, the lowest level of voter turnout since 1978.[7] Even before we consider turnout there is a pretty significant gap. Registered voters represent a much smaller share of potential voters in the United States than just about any other OECD country: Only about 65% of the U.S. voting-age population (and 71% of the voting-age citizenry) is registered, according to the Census Bureau, compared with 96% in Sweden and 93% in the United Kingdom.[8]

This isn't just about voting, of course — we have to consider what happens after the results of elections are tallied. The people who are elected help to shape the policies that govern how our society works. Voting gaps end up being a significant factor in biasing public policy against a large majority of Americans, which includes large numbers of low-income households, and in favor of the comparatively tiny group consisting of the most affluent households — those who don't vote versus those who do. In other words, when people don't vote, it also means they often aren't as well represented on important matters as those who do participate. Closing voting gaps is significant not only for strengthening the integrity of our electoral system but for achieving a democracy that improves the lives of all Americans.

Rather than try to measure any of these things in absolute terms, or even to quantify them, let's focus on closing the gaps. Think about it this way: the number of people who are registered to vote — unless we get 100% eligible participation — is just evidence of failure. Remove the judgment from the way we measure entirely and it's not about the "right" ideas at all, but insuring that we are seeing maximum diversity in the ideas that are being generated.

We need to use and apply our imagination to address a problem like voter participation. Incremental improvements to the system or slight upticks in participation are not going to be sufficient. There are lots of ideas and proposed solutions to solve for these issues, but are they the ones that we need to make progress toward a better future? Are we thinking about the long-term impacts of these issues, or just identifying things what feels like the priority right now?

How we do ensure we are getting new, ambitious ideas for solving this type of problem? The more collisions there are between people, the more ideas are exchanged and the greater likelihood that even more interesting things will emerge. We need to open up the conversation, and use our imagination.

A key part of the equation is the randomness of the encounter. If you put a group of people are put together in a room and tell them to generate ideas, questions, and new opinions, with no criticism allowed, before long you will get a long list of ideas. Everybody has contributed; nobody has been criticized. But the overwhelming majority of those ideas and questions are superficial. Most brainstorming sessions actually inhibit the productivity of the group. We become less than the sum of our parts.

Instead of manufacturing the collisions, what if you increased the chances for the random encounters? In Slough, the individual behaviors of the small group didn't translate to broad-based changes in behavior or attitude among others in the community.

But if the entire community had been part of the experience, would things have gone differently?

Tony Hsieh, the founder of Zappos, is trying to prove that you can engineer a community in a way that increases the number of collisions, and produces a range of benefits — from increased innovation potential to greater levels of happiness. The Downtown Project, as he calls it, is an effort to transform Las Vegas into a hyper-efficient generator of new ideas, innovation, and business energy. Hsieh has calculated that he spends "1,000 collisionable hours" annually in downtown Las Vegas — where Zappos is headquartered. These collisions, essentially serendipitous encounters, result in unexpected conversations, cross-pollination of ideas, sharing of experiences and more — all of which Hsieh argues is a good thing and he'd like to see more people in his company and the community having them ... Such random encounters increase innovation and productivity. The Downtown Project is designed to "institutionalize [that] return on luck."[9]

Reprogramming the Operating System

We can learn a lot about how geography has shaped our perception of creativity and imagination — but only through a historical lens. The human brain has imagination built into its operating system. We are hard wired to dream up things that are not always directly connected to the world that we experience today. Not some of us. Everyone. The brains of the people living in different parts of the world are not different — but the environment in which they live may influence whether people use their imagination or not.

For most casual computer users, there is little appeal to updating to a new operating system. Not only does it take a while to get the handle on all the features of the most current operating system, but the so-called improvements offered in a newer version are not always evident. But that upgrade is important. At some point, the age of our computer's operating system is going to start blocking us off from the rest of the world. Our files and programs won't be compatible with what everyone else is using. We'll find ourselves envious of the speed, new features, and slick look of friends' updated computers.

Moving away from a singularly focused line of thinking around innovation — and the incremental, constant updates that it encourages — requires us to update the system software in our brain. It requires that we use a new version of the tools that govern how we work, engage and talk about imagination across every sector of our society. The current system is out of date.

In 1936, Alan Turing published a paper where he imagined in precise detail a computing machine. Turing is credited as the father of computer science — his paper is generally regarded as the first appearance of the modern idea of a computer. And during World War II, Turing had a real computing machine built that played an important part in decrypting German military and naval signals, and so in the defeat of Nazism. What he imagined became the reality of the world of computational power. Turing himself famously said "Sometimes it is the people who no one imagines anything of who do the things that no one can imagine."

What exactly did Turing imagine his machine being able to do? In the paper, he described a theoretical operation that used an infinitely long piece of tape containing a series of symbols. A machine could read the symbols on the tape as well as add its own symbols. It could move about to different parts of the tape, one symbol at a time.

The world had plenty of pretty sophisticated adding machines that would allow someone to perform simple calculations. What Turing offered was the idea of a general-purpose programmable machine — so you could provide the machine with a program and it would do what the program specified.

But he didn't stop here. In 1950 Turing published a paper called "Computing machinery and intelligence."[10] He believed that computers would become so powerful that they would think — like humans. He predicted that by the year 2000 the concept of artificial intelligence would be a reality. To prove his point, he devised the Turing Test: which would have a judge sitting at a computer terminal typing questions to two entities, one a person and the other a computer. The judge would be asked to decide which entity was human and which the computer based on their responses. If the judge is wrong the computer passed the Turing Test and was considered intelligent. This concept was dismissed as crazy, possibly even dangerous. And while Artificial Intelligence did not full become integrated into our lives by the turn of the century as Turing predicted, it is very much a reality today.

What differentiated Alan Turing from other potentially influential thinkers was his ability to program his idea — to actually build the machine that he had imagined. For anyone whose imagination produces a new and ambitious idea — being able to turn that from concept into reality can be the difference between success and failure.

The thing to keep in mind is this: the people and organizations that stand out for their ability to both turn an idea into a tangible product (or similar), or have an intentional impact on society, are not only better — they're intentionally different. In every situation where someone has offered a new and different idea, the usual response is "That's just not how it's done." Sticking to a formula that simply repeats what has been done previously — even if you do it faster, bigger, or more colorfully, will always run its course. That approach will only get you so far, and that won't be anywhere as close to extraordinary as it could be if you started with an idea, born from imagination, that is beyond what we recognize is possible today.

Change When You Don't Expect It

Humans are creatures of habit — or more appropriately perhaps, creatures of patterns. Getting to work on time in the morning is the result of recognizing patterns in your daily commute and responding to changes in schedule and traffic. You are able to sense that you are coming down with a cold because how you feel normally has been disrupted. No matter the situation, work or personal, recognizing the patterns faster than anyone else is what provides you with the edge, in survival or competition. Add in powerful algorithms and computer programs, be it from Google or IBM Watson (the world's most powerful supercomputer), and the ability to identify and analyze patterns is more powerful than ever.

We must be mindful of the patterns that exist in our lives, because the more predictable we become, the more likely we are to stop using our imagination. The future of intelligence, and more specifically artificial intelligence, is based on making our patterns better. The idea is to use "selective attention" — to focus on what really matters so that poor selections are removed before they ever hit the conscious brain. And while the algorithms that make our work increasingly efficient, eliminate errors, and even begin to anticipate or recommend what we might want to consider — it also eliminates the most valuable ingredient in our imagination: uncertainty. Remember that our imagination fires most when we are uncomfortable. Breaking patterns makes people uncomfortable. And you need to get comfortable being uncomfortable.

Noah Brier, an entrepreneur and founder of Percolate, was taught very early the benefits of breaking pattern — and has never forgotten. "Do you remember playing with blocks at school when you were in kindergarten? I remember working with blocks – and we had a little workbook that offered different shapes and patterns we could build. It was all about learning counting and math and whatever. I remember finishing the book and so I was screwing around. The teacher, she could tell I was bored. So, she came back to where I was playing," and she said, "If you are bored, why don't you just flip the book over and start from the back?"[11] That guidance showed Brier that the traditional approach to something, the accepted practice, does not have to be accepted at all — there are an unlimited number of options that could be explored.

The breakthrough moments when your imagination offers up a new idea can happen without warning. When you get up in the middle of a meeting and go to the bathroom, it's likely to return having formed some breakthrough idea or interesting question. When you get in your car and drive down the highway, only to have your head flood with questions and thoughts. There is science to back up that reality. When we stop trying to come up with ideas, or complete specific tasks, we provide our brain with an opportunity to change its focus — and our imagination goes wild as a result. What exactly is happening? Two things to note:

(1) Intense focus on something has its limitations. The human brain just wasn't built for extended focus, so making a point to give your brain time to rest ultimately will make it more effective.

(2) Our brains have two modes: the "focused mode" which we use when we're learning something, and "diffuse mode," which is our more relaxed, day-dreamy mode when we're not trying to think so hard. When you're focusing, you're actually blocking your access to the diffuse mode. The new, interesting things emerge from your brain when in diffuse mode.

We have to use that time to actually give our brain the space to function differently. We need to change our environment. Some options to consider:

- Take a walk — outside.

- Close your eyes (maybe even power nap).

- Listen to music.

- Talk to someone.

- Take a shower.

Taking a five-minute break and getting away from technology and work, giving your brain a few moments of rest, and catch up on things can yield remarkable results. The most important consideration is to change your physical environment, ever so slightly, so that your overall experience is different.

The Least Funny Comedian of All Time

One profession that requires you to be comfortable with being uncomfortable is comedy. Harrison Greenbaum is very funny. He understands exactly what it takes to succeed as a professional standup comedian and humor writer — how much work is required for someone to fulfill their peak humor potential, and how to strike the right balance between process and imagination. As he explained it, comedians have to think constantly about how to push themselves, and their humor, to the point where they don't know if it will work. When you create a joke there a process — every comedian follows the same recipe. What makes a joke funny are the special ingredients that get mixed in along the way.

Greenbaum explains the process required to create humor this way: "We come up with a joke and then do it every single night on stage, three times a night, with different people listening, in different settings, to see how it affects the audience. Every time I tell a joke I get some response and then I tweak the language, the delivery, something to try and make it better. Maybe I take a word out, or change the timing. I keep changing and editing it and morphing it until it kills consistently." While the core of the process never changes, every comedian has to integrate their own ingredients. There are no limits to the number of different ingredients that Greenbaum, or any comedian, can integrate to produce a guaranteed laugh, or a routine full of jokes that, night after night, performance after performance, will resonate with the audience.

The worst thing a comedian can do, Greenbaum warns, is fall into a pattern where he or she gets comfortable — only playing to audiences that have historically embraced their humor, or using the exact same set of jokes night after night without considering what impact a different venue or medium might have. "The comics who hunt to find where their jokes are funniest and stops there tend to become really unfunny," Greenbaum told me.[12] In fact, if all someone does is follow the process steps, and never uses their imagination or considers ways to integrate their own personal ingredients, chances are they will end up as the least funny comedian of all time.

Peter McGaw, author of *The Humor Code*, studies what makes people laugh. He told me there are provable patterns that can be used to structure humor, noting that the things that we tend to find humorous in the world have three conditions occurring:

> One, the situation is in some way wrong, unsettling, confusing, threatening — what we call a violation. At the same time, simultaneously, that's the second condition, it's seen as somehow okay, safe, or acceptable, what we call benign. So it's these benign violations, these things that are confusing yet make sense, that are threatening yet safe, that are wrong yet okay that create this psychological experience.
>
> One way that you can help make a threatening situation more safe is for it to be psychologically distant from the audience. For instance, you can have the situation happen to someone you don't care about or even someone you don't like. That helps make it benign. Or it could have happened a long time ago so you can avoid the kind of too soon comedy fail but waiting enough time for this thing to sort of fade a little bit, for it to be a little less emotionally rousing. Or it could happen on the other side of the world. It could be spatially distant. It could be far, far away. It's definitely easier to laugh at tragedies on the other side of the planet than it is to laugh at tragedies in your own backyard.[13]
>
> The last way you can do this is for this thing to be hypothetical — not to be based in reality. And so violations that are not based in reality are much easier to laugh at than violations that are typically based in reality, especially when those violations are really big like the ones in "South Park" and "The Simpsons" and "Family Guy" and so on.

People's ability to transport themselves into worlds that don't really exist is fundamental to the creation of comedy. People can suspend disbelief and imagine situations happening even though they aren't really happening. "Nothing is really happening in 'Family Guy,'" McGraw noted. "It's just a story being told and someone drawing pictures. It also occurs on a smaller scale — when people believe that a priest, a rabbi, and whatever the third person is walk into a bar. They believe that those people would be together, in a bar no less. You can take these very fanciful situations and be affected by them."

Computer scientists have used the patterns around humor to try and create robots that can write and deliver jokes as well as humans. As an article in *The New York Times* acknowledged, however, "The cognitive processes that cause people to snicker at this sort of one-liner are only partly understood, which makes it all the more difficult for computers to mimic them. Unlike, say, chess, which is grounded in a fixed set of rules, there are no hard-and-fast formulas for comedy. To get around that cognitive complexity, computational humor researchers have by and large taken a more concrete approach: focusing on simple linguistic relationships, like double meanings, rather than on trying to model the high-level mental mechanics that underlie humor."[14]

Thus far, the computers have not been able to develop better humor than the humans. The goal that Alan Turing mapped out more than half a century ago has still not been achieved. The reason? Computers are human inventions and programmed by humans, so they are limited by how the programmers use their imagination in creating the computer from the start. While the computers are trying to identify and follow the patterns, human comedians are constantly changing patterns, performing different shows in front of different audiences. Even if they repeat performances in the same location, with the same audience in some cases, the world has changed and the perception of a joke will be different. As the comedians are constantly changing patterns, the jokes change.

Even Peter McGraw acknowledged to me that, "a big part of this stuff it still ends up being the lonely person just working hard on their own, banging their head against the wall so to speak." He then added "well, that's not totally true. I do think that some level of engagement and enjoying yourself enhances this."

There is a myth that ideas — anything tied to imagination really — are only useful at the beginning, before something becomes real and tangible. Imagination (and creativity for that matter) is therefore confined to the planning stage. And, when something emerges from the imagination, it is pure and valuable — but then can get derailed along the way to becoming a reality by the response that others offer, the limitations that are imposed by people who are wedded to existing ways of operating, and more.

The myth, according to Josh Linkner, is that "once the idea is launched then imagination is no longer even needed. That after an idea is formed everything else is just about being in heads-down execution mode." That premise is totally false. "Getting an idea to begin with requires imagination, but so does executing it. You may have a big idea to cure cancer in some unique way, but then to execute that idea requires another thousand ideas or micro imagination steps to navigate through all the challenges that you have yet to encounter. Imagination is not just a requirement only up front."[15]

Linkner is correct. Imagination is a requirement through the entire process, from the initial creation and suggestion of an idea all the way through execution and beyond. There isn't a set path or procedure to follow; imagination must be applied continuously and in different ways, at different points. There is no single, measurable outcome that can be measured in relation to using and applying imagination. The only thing we know for sure is that whatever rules and structures we are using now to encourage and govern the use of imagination are not working to unlock the full potential of our imagination. We need to use our imagination to figure out how to use our imagination even more.

Challenge: Rewrite History

Every moment of every day influences the course of our lives. Our experiences and perspectives are shaped by the events of the past. What would happen if certain events had turned out differently? What if Bill Buckner had fielded the ball hit to him cleanly and gotten the out in the 1986 World Series? What if you had missed your train to work yesterday? What would have happened if …?

To Do: Take a historical event — something specific to your life, or something that happened in the world — and imagine a different outcome. Rewrite history as if life had proceeded down a different path. What would have changed? What would be different?

Challenge: Build Something

Building something can trigger your imagination. But not so much when you are building something outlined for you. You need a variety of materials to open up the full range of possibilities. If you have an unlimited number of pieces to build with, you have an unlimited number of options.

To Do: Grab a few LEGO bricks. Start building. Something. Anything. Everything.

NOTES

1. Weiner, E. *The Geography of Bliss*. Twelve, January 5, 2009. http://www.ericweinerbooks.com/books/the-geography-of-bliss/description/
2. *Making Slough Happy*. BBC. http://www.bbc.co.uk/pressoffice/pressreleases/stories/2005/10_october/25/slough.shtml
3. Weiner, E. *The Geography of Genius*. Simon & Schuster, January 5, 2016. http://www.ericweinerbooks.com/books/the-geography-of-genius/description/
4. Why innovation thrives in cities. MIT — June 4, 2013. http://news.mit.edu/2013/why-innovation-thrives-in-cities-0604

5. http://givingusa.org/giving-usa-2015-press-release-giving-usa-americans-donated-an-estimated-358-38-billion-to-charity-in-2014-highest-total-in-reports-60-year-history/
6. http://www.pewresearch.org/fact-tank/2015/05/06/u-s-voter-turnout-trails-most-developed-countries/
7. Who votes? Congressional elections and the American electorate: 1978–2014. U.S. *Census Bureau.* https://www.census.gov/content/dam/Census/library/publications/2015/demo/p20-577.pdf
8. http://www.pewresearch.org/fact-tank/2016/08/02/u-s-voter-turnout-trails-most-developed-countries/
9. http://www.forbes.com/sites/techonomy/2013/11/15/why-zappos-ceo-hsieh-wants-to-enable-more-collisions-in-vegas/
10. Turing, A.M. (1950). Computing machinery and intelligence. *Mind, 49,* 433–460. http://www.csee.umbc.edu/courses/471/papers/turing.pdf
11. Interview with Noah Brier — September 14, 2015.
12. Interview with Harrison Greenbaum — June 16, 2016.
13. Interview with Peter McGaw — October 25, 2015.
14. Stone, A. Can Computers be Funny? *The New York Times* — January 4, 2013. http://www.nytimes.com/2013/01/06/opinion/sunday/can-computers-be-funny.html
15. Interview with Josh Linkner — July 29, 2015.

All Hands on Deck

9

To close the Imagination Gap we will need to work together. This chapter explains how a "war room" style approach encourages and enables people to use and apply imagination. Each set of activities builds on the next by providing results that inform future interactions. Everything is agile and iterative, and the operation is organized to maximize every opportunity to learn and adapt in real time.

Stop Overthinking the Way You Think Things Are Supposed to Be

In 2002, Stanford professor Robert I. Sutton wrote a book entitled *Weird Ideas that Work*[1] that was designed to help organizations find new and better ways to generate creative thinking. Sutton had studied some of the most innovative people and companies in the world and concluded that what works for routine work does not when it comes to creative outputs. His overarching recommendation was to take everything that we know about business and do the opposite.

Sutton offered a dozen recommendations, but also noted in doing so that he did not necessarily believe in the ideas, or have faith that they would be successful when implemented. Instead, he suggested each individual or organization figures out what worked best for them and merely offered his ideas for where they might start. Ironically, though not all that surprisingly, many of Sutton's "Weird Rules" became standard practice in companies that were trying to embrace and foster innovation. We are much more likely to take Sutton's ideas than generate our own. Many of the ideas that Sutton originally championed, once mainstreamed, lose their edginess and purpose — exactly the opposite of what he counseled in his book.

The very situation that Sutton set out to tackle with his book — and arguably was temporarily successful in disrupting — is now back. Yes, companies are now doing different things than they were nearly two decades ago when Sutton's book was first published. But, they are all doing the same different things. On the plus side, after time has passed and circumstances have changed weird ideas still seem just as scary and confusing. What was once weird can become weird again.

I went back to look at Sutton's ideas and found two that could still inspire individuals and organizations to use their imagination more in their work. They are:

- **Find some happy people and get them to fight.** Management experts all agree that a work environment free of conflict will produce the best work. But we all know that in any organization there are disagreements that might be better aired. Getting smart people to vigorously debate their ideas, Sutton would argue, is one of the quickest methods to expose flaws and push people to think beyond their current experiences.

- **Ignore people who have solved the exact problem you face.** There is a bias in favor of hiring people who have done similar work or who have been successful on similar assignments in the past. If your goal is to achieve the exact same outcome as someone else, that's a reasonable thought process to follow — but if you expect anything different, you are best to bring a different expertise to bear.

What Sutton's "Weird Rules" do more than anything is provide a reminder that one of the best things an organization can do is throw out the rule book. And to take that thought process even further, every time a new rule book gets created, consider yourself invited to throw it out as well. The more we change up our routines, the more we can resist the temptation to create "best practices" and build systems to the point that we stop using our imagination and lose our edge (again).

If you have expectations about the way things are supposed to be, you're constantly going to be comparing whatever you are doing to what you think should be and you'll inevitably be disappointed. The whole idea of closing the imagination gap is that you will be in a position to constantly come up with better ways of doing things, and never stop working toward realizing that vision.

"Having expectations is a mind killer," Rita J. King told me. "Everything and everybody is a work in progress. Nothing is a static, fixed reality. As soon as you see everything, including yourself, as a work in progress, you begin to realize that you have contributions that you can make toward improving reality."[2]

Imagination, when applied, gives us all the ability to navigate equally well between the tangible and concrete and the nebulous. The things we know and the things we can't know because they don't exist yet. The ability to look at a lot of things, make sense of them in our own way, and always be looking to change them further is the most special talent of all.

"I think that people can be imaginative all they want; it's when they start making it public the question becomes 'are they going to get judged and how do they deal with that?'" Peter Shankman told me. "Sometimes when they do make it public and they get judged poorly they tend to not want to do it anymore; it scares them off …. And if you start putting limits on it then it's no longer imagination."[3]

The War Room Approach

Abraham Lincoln had a dedicated room in the White House where he would meet with advisers and communicate via telegraph with his Civil War generals and other officers to keep tabs of what was going on at the battlefront. Winston Churchill had secure offices built beneath Whitehall, the home of the British Intelligence Service, where he and his cabinet ministers could meet to strategize during WWII. But it wasn't until early 1990s that the term and use of "war rooms" became an organizational strategy, as well as part of popular culture.

In 1993, *The War Room* a documentary that showed the behind the scenes workings of Bill Clinton's successful campaign for President, was nominated for an Academy Award. Until the film, a rapid-response operation was considered an exotic concept. Or as the film's producer told *The New York Times* in 2008, "People didn't like to think of elections as wars, which of course they are."[4] Today, many different types of organizations employ some variation on a war room in the hopes of emulating the energy and effectiveness that is found at the heart of a sophisticated political operation.

The political war room gathers the core decision-makers for a campaign in one room or in close proximity allowing the campaign to make decisions and act quickly when they see a threat or opportunity. There are other orientations where media activity for a campaign is monitored around the clock to help feed rapid-response efforts. And on Election Day, it is common for campaigns to build a war room operation to oversee get-out-the-vote effects, and keep track of turnout, exit polls, and other factors that could impact the outcome of a race.

The key ingredient in a war room is proximity. Instead of toiling in separate offices, the core team sits together in one big, open room, outfitted with central worktables, whiteboards, and flip charts to facilitate group discussions. Screens cover every surface, delivering news, data, and whatever else the campaign needs to track happenings in real time. War rooms are intended to be catalysts for decision-making, and they do this by keeping the most important people in the operation together so that information flows readily and actions can be taken quickly. Political campaigns are also designed to cascade — with each set of activities building on the next and a constant stream of results and analysis being used to keep short-term and long-term plans updated. The work is designed to be agile and iterative, and every element of the operation beyond the war room is organized to maximize the learning in real time. The organ that powers that type of operation lives in the war room.

What does a "war room" have to do with imagination? A war room approach relies on imagination. There are no fixed plans that dictate every action. War rooms are not conveyer belts for decision-making. Rather, they are designed to function when the situation is fluid, the need to think quickly, not to mention differently, is at a premium. It is the setup that will prevent an organization, and all those who work for it, from falling into the patterns that keep them from tapping into their imagination. Organizations should not build innovation labs or imagination hubs — designated areas where the expectation is that people will gather to generate new ideas. Instead, they should create war rooms that are designed to adapt to any situation or scenario as it unfolds, making sure that the organization never gets stuck in a pattern again.

Your imagination is always active. You are always capable of generating ideas and pushing beyond what your current experience suggests is possible. But you need to create an environment where your imagination can be applied — continuously, not at a particular moment or on demand. A war room is designed without a formal structure. It doesn't have committees or departments. It's all hands on deck. Everyone involved in the operation has a role. Everyone shares responsibility when it comes to learning and considering what's possible. Everyone is expected to be part of figuring out how best to craft plans and advocate for how things should be done.

Dwight Eisenhower famously said "In preparing for battle I have always found that plans are useless, but planning is indispensable." Our imagination provides you a powerful tool for planning and pursuing the future. And you can do that from inside the war room.

Centrifugal Workforce

Centrifugal force is defined as "the apparent force, equal and opposite to the centripetal force, drawing a rotating body away from the center of rotation, caused by the inertia of the body."[5] That force is ubiquitous in our lives. We don't sit around thinking about it, measuring it, or probably pay it much mind whatsoever. But it's there. We experience it when we round a corner in a car or when an airplane banks into a turn. We see it in the spin cycle of a washing machine or when children ride on a merry-go-round. An explanation with less science jargon might go as follows: if you are observing something spinning from the outside, you see an inward force acting to constrain the thing that is rotating to a circular path. But if you are part of the rotating system, your experience is the opposite and the centrifugal force will push you away from the center of the circle.

When things start to spin, centrifugal force is what pushes everything out from the center to the edges. If you think about it, the same force can be applied to ideas — making sure that new and different ways of thinking about the future are pushed out to the furthest reaches of an organization or community. They can't be allowed to only stay in the middle (or at the top) of an organization. In real life, we can't resist centrifugal force — it just happens. We need to stop trying to resist those forces and instead apply them to our businesses and organizations. We need to harness centrifugal force.

The first step is to hire a centrifugal workforce.

Every organization should be encouraging new and different ideas to spread. Imagination can't be the domain of only a small group or assigned to one division or department, nor can it be contained within one community. The willingness to consider an entirely different future doesn't thrive at the heart of an operation, it gains strength as more people know about it and start to buy in.

There are all sorts of models of how things spread, and they're often incompatible with each other. There's no typical way in which things become popular. It's hard to be exposed to one particular idea because there's just so much other stuff to pay attention to. And while things are able to rise above the noise so that more people pay attention to it, those situations are extraordinarily rare, somewhat arbitrary, and still miss a lot of people.

While it is true we live in a connected world, in which technology is accessible to (almost) everyone and information has the potential to spread (almost) everywhere, the reality is different. Most information does not come anywhere close to reaching the masses. Algorithms, which are increasingly used to personalize experiences and prioritize what we see and hear, are based on our past actions (and what our likes, shares, and clicks suggest we want to see more of), and continually narrow the focus of what we experience online. And, we have become so attached to media and technology to spread information that we often fail to consider how informal information networks, perceptions about information from different sources and channels, and the impact of information transmitted through word of mouth influence how information spreads.

Sometimes it is the ideas that provide clear incentives or compelling benefits that seem to spread more easily. For people to accept information there must be trust, authenticity, relevance, and salience in the message, messenger, and medium. We often hear that the "best idea" wins, but who decides those ideas are best also influences who is willing to consider them in the first place. And with social media, when something receives more likes it also gets more exposure, which opens it up to receive more likes. Audiences say they care most about the quality of the media they are consuming, but the systems that help media to spread are powered by other factors.

One thing is clear: if we want information to spread, we need to help it spread. It won't happen on its own. Spreading information requires a commitment to having more people in on the conversation. It also requires an organized effort where people actively push information to the outer edges, instead of keeping them close to the center. That runs counter to our current experience and how so much of media, software, and organizations are designed to function.

The roles and responsibilities of a centrifugal workforce prioritize sharing and spreading of information with the clear goal of information going as far away from the center as possible. Each person must be capable of spreading information and take responsibility for organizing and supporting the sharing of everything — insights, expertise, data, whatever. Share it all. Push it out as far as possible.

How Do You Hire for Imagination?

If your goal is to use and apply imagination more in your organization, where should you go looking for those types of skills — and what exactly are you looking for? On most job descriptions, you will find a list of attributes to help match the right person to the position. For more "creative" roles you will often find skills including "strategic imagination" or "big idea generating ability" as requirements. If the role is technical in nature, the list will include experience working on certain technical platforms or comfort programming in certain languages.

The characteristics that are often attributed to people who use their imagination include: they daydream, they work the hours that work for them, they spend time alone, they express themselves — in any number of ways — and they constantly shake things up. Not only won't you find those on most job descriptions, they are often perceived as negative qualities. They translate in practical ways as: the person can't keep a set schedule, they dress in unconventional ways, they don't always play well with others, and more. Nobody wants to hire someone who displays those tendencies.

Those characteristics make people nervous because we face an imagination gap. We are more likely to accept what we have known, including what characteristics define someone who has been successful, instead of thinking about how the makeup of the person might align with the future you haven't yet figured out. People who have held creative roles before will get hired for them again. People who have technical experience will get tapped for roles building apps and similar tools. But whether or not they know how to use or apply their imagination is never fully considered.

Macky Alston believes that you can't identify someone with an active imagination through a traditional interview process.

"I wouldn't ask them anything," he told me, suggesting that the answer people provide are often designed to present an image that aligns with a traditional definition of success. "I look at them. If they dress like everybody else I'm less interested in them. If they are already manifesting in the canvas that is their body, non-conformity, but not for non-conformity's sake, but for self-expression, that's interesting to me." Alston says "he looks for evidence of freedom, un-inhibition."[6]

Alston says you can learn a lot about an applicant by how they talk about the defining experiences in their life. While everyone has stories of hardship and overcoming difficulty, and well-prepared applicants will offer evidence of leadership and resilience, the people who stand out to Alston are those who have bucked the social norms and pressures. Alston has found that the common denominator among the most compelling people he has worked with are that they all moments of radical nonconformity. "In Deuteronomy there is this text where we are called to choose life, not death, blessing not curse, and the understanding between God and God's people is that in the end humans either decide to be members or the walking dead or to live lives of non-conformity."

Bradley Feinstein, cofounder and president at Dropel Fabrics, says "the fundamental difference between those that know how to use and apply their imagination and those that don't is that they take a shot." The evidence that their imagination has been engaged is in how they show they are thinking and applying their experiences. "Most of my friends went into very traditional careers out of college – doctors, lawyers, finance, consulting. We all learned different frameworks, we all learned how to think. And that's the most valuable thing. I think we need to do a better job showing the value of the experience and the path, rather than just the outcome."[7]

Sree Sreenivasan, the former Chief Digital Office for the Metropolitan Museum of Art, says that it is that willingness to explore that is most important when hiring talented people into an organization. Specifically, he uses it to find applicants who have the greatest potential to use and apply their imagination. "What we are looking for, even in our coders and people who are doing our tech work, is that they are willing to be inspired by what they have around them. They have to think that their job isn't to just come and execute what they know already but to be open to new things they haven't thought of and to do it in this place of amazing opportunity."[8]

Over the past few years, Goldman Sachs has been analyzing its employees in an attempt to identify what skills and experiences would best support their work. Jake Siewert told me "when we looked at people who do well here, what traits they have in common — it doesn't correlate to schools as you'd rank them. It doesn't correlate to GPA. It correlates to a lot of things that you'd consider less tangible that are a little harder to spot." For example, the firm prizes teamwork, he told me, so "people who do well in sports, particularly team sports, tend to do pretty well here." That's not surprising.

What might work for any organization looking to hire people who can use and apply their imagination? There is no standardized test for imagination or degree you can earn that qualifies you to work for an organization that embraces new ideas and forward thinking — nor should there be. Imagination is part of every discipline, field of academic study, and professional role. We should not be satisfied with just considering people who self-identify as highly imaginative, especially because the pool of people who believe that is presently quite small. So, how do you assess whether someone has the ability to dream — with or without some specific purpose? What questions should you be asking in a job interview?

"In the world of comedy the best predictor that someone is funny is intelligence. Some people think creative ability predicts comic ability but the problem with that is that intelligence predicts creative ability," explained Peter McGraw. "It's someone who's a little bit optimistic about life and someone who just generally naturally has positive emotion, that kind of thing"[9] that are most likely to produce humor that others appreciate and enjoy.

Dia Simms told me, "There are people who just have a lot of ideas which is an expression of imagination. That actually to me presents itself pretty clearly and quickly in the workplace if you are asking the right questions. There are always your obvious go to people. If I ask them a question, they extemporaneously can give me thirty ideas; maybe they are not all great, but they are idea machines."[10] At the same time, Simms suggested it is more important to have somebody who is broadly imaginative. That type of person can take information, even a limited amount of information (sometimes it is better when they have less information because they won't have the preconstraints that won't allow them to be as imaginative as possible), and make something amazing out of it. "I think it's no different than a star quarterback; it feels like it is their clear prowess to come up with novel concepts. People around them will be a little bit like flashlights in the sun." Those people, Simms stresses, are not easy to find, so when you do it's really quite obvious.

Recognizing Is Acknowledging

Once you have hired the right people, your work is just beginning. Most people will do most of what they are told. They assume the position they are assigned and act accordingly. "When we are told to play a certain role, we think that is the only role we are supposed to play," Noah Brier, the founder of Percolate, told me. "We think we are the designer, or we are the engineer. And when we think we need to be the engineer, or the designer no matter what. We overplay our hand. As the designer I might think nobody else can do what I do, and when it comes to engineering I probably defer too much to someone else because I assume they know better."[11]

Brier believes that every role, and every employee, has some responsibility to the operation as a whole — but acknowledges that most organizations design roles and structures so that isn't possible. While organizations say they want people to collaborate, they often make it difficult for people to mesh their talents. That is true with the physical setup of an office, where different departments and teams are kept in separate areas, as well as in the management structure, where different roles are managed and measured by different standards. When it comes to recognizing and acknowledging imagination in people, or the capacity for them to play a more "creative" role within an organization, organizations must be especially careful not to let structure or bias influence their thinking.

Johanna Schwartz told me that when she was in film school, and now as a professional filmmaker, it's quite common for her to be pushed toward a role that is more organizational than creative. "I love organizing and I love my spreadsheets to be tidy. But that doesn't mean that I don't have imagination and that doesn't mean that I can't be creative and it doesn't mean I can't be a good filmmaker," she told me. "People would see how organized I was and they would just assume that I should be playing an organizational role. It's as if people didn't think that you could be both organized and creative. There is this weird belief that have to be this haphazard, disheveled, lost inside your own mind creative type in order to be a great filmmaker. But the truth is, you can have a very neat desk and produce extraordinary films as well."[12]

Whatever bias exists in our society also influences how organizations are structured, and how different employees are assessed. Since our imagination spins out ideas that are not understood, or that people aren't comfortable with, the people who use and apply their imagination most are often considered to be more difficult to manage. Industries that are most often associated with creativity and imagination also suffer from bias, and reflect the existence of the imagination gap, by continually tapping people who are perceived to have the best creative attributes, leading to a more narrow and less diverse workforce. A few statistics for context are given here:

- A study by *Campaign* magazine and the Institute of Practitioners in Advertising found that fewer than a third of chairs or chief executives of advertising agencies are female, and in creative departments, women make up less than a quarter of the leadership.[13]

– Silicon Valley's tech workers are overwhelmingly male (83%) who are white or Asian (94%). At Google, a company that has made a very public effort to improve its diversity, 81% of technical roles are held by men, with 57% held by whites, 37% by Asians, and only 3% by Hispanics, and 1% by Blacks. Only a quarter of the senior leadership roles are held by women; Hispanics (2%) and Blacks (1%) are barely represented at all (Whites holding 70% of those roles and Asians 25% of them).[14]

Study after study reflects the value of having a diverse corporate workforce, because diverse insights offer better results, particularly when it comes to imagination and creativity. There are measurable financial benefits. One study stated, "if two companies are identical in every way except for racial/ethnic diversity and female representation in leadership, the more diverse company will, in all likelihood, have higher revenues, be more profitable, and have a higher market value."[15]

Is gender bias so prevalent in our society that it even influences who we consider to have a strong imagination, or be capable of creative thought? Apparently, yes. Devon Proudfoot, a PhD candidate at Duke, and her colleagues Aaron Kay and Christy Koval conducted multiple studies on gender bias. The results suggested that men were considered to be more creative,[16] and that men and women associated creativity with stereotypically "masculine" traits such as independence and risk-taking and not "feminine" traits, such as cooperativeness and sensitivity. Even the study was biased!

In an interview with *Harvard Business Review*, Dr. Proudfoot explained further:

> Our research clearly showed that people associate creativity with … masculine qualities—boldness, risk taking, independence. And because of this, people believe that men are generally more creative than women. It doesn't affect just assessments of work, like an architect's design. We also found that the bosses of 134 executives

rated women as significantly less creative in their thinking than men. That has repercussions: In another study we did, male managers who were rated as more creative than female managers were perceived as more deserving of rewards.[17]

There is general agreement that challenging the status quo requires autonomy and independence — but there is no evidence to suggest that men are more capable or willing to exhibit those traits than women. There is also no evidence that male and female brains generate imaginative ideas differently. We each have our own unique imagination that is shaped by our experiences and the inputs we received. Since gender has nothing to do with how our imagination works, so the only explanation as to why men are considered more creative than women is because of sexism.

In my research for this book, I reviewed dozens of lists of the "most creative" and "most innovative" people and found significantly more men listed than women — almost twice as many in most cases. Anecdotally, many of the women who were included on those lists were recognized more for having a high-ranking position in a seemingly creative organization (an advertising agency, consumer brand, or tech startup) and not for a specific idea or innovation that they helped to create. I have also met, and interviewed, countless women who have extraordinary ideas that are not recognized, while men have routinely been celebrated for what appears to be less imaginative contributions.

I asked Dia Simms if she thought there were different standards when it comes to who is considered imaginative or not. She said "well, if we are talking about the United States, there are going to be very few compilation lists — unless it is Black History Month — that have a lot of black women on them. That is an American problem, in terms of minorities of color are just not being well represented." She offered two reasons for this:

First, you are not going to be at the selection committee. It is unfortunate at this point in time but its true. And second, the things that they may be doing to be creative may not be recognized with the same level of merit, that the likely predominantly white male institution doing the voting is doing.

Obviously there are black women across many socio-economic classes, but those who are strapped for cash, or living in a single family household or any of those realities. I promise you are the most creative you will ever meet. That is a fact. They are the reality that exists around Hyperloop (Elon Musk's idea for a tube-system to transport people from coast to coast in a fraction of the time required for air travel), or figuring out a way to grow flowers out of your fireplace type of crazy imagination.[18]

This is an important criticism of the entire conversation about imagination and creativity — and in many ways how it is disconnected from the reality of the world. The awards that are given out for and the recognition that is paid toward the most innovative products and companies today is symptomatic of the lack of real diversity and understanding in a lot of the world. "I hate to show my junior psychology undergraduate degree," Simms told me, "but this goes back to the basic hierarchy of needs. If you are disenfranchised, if your safety is at risk on a regular basis, you are not sure about how you are going to eat and the basic ills of society that we are all familiar with, getting to the point of freeing your mind to think of cool ideas all ideas all day is going to be nearly impossible."

There are clearly issues of access, privilege, misogyny, and systemic racism that influence who are put in positions to offer new ideas, and which ideas are seriously considered and pursued. Not only is imagination key to addressing these core issues, but the potential for more people to use and apply imagination will continue to be limited as long as these barriers exist. Again, everyone has a unique imagination, and the more and more diverse, the community of people who are encouraged to use and apply their imagination becomes, the more we can expect new and groundbreaking ideas to emerge.

An Asset Is an Asset Is an Asset

No matter what industry we consider, imagination is going to be among your most valuable assets. "There is imagination everywhere, absolutely everywhere," Johanna Schwartz suggests. Of course, to find who is using and applying your imagination will require some effort. Schwartz believes that you should look for people who have an open mind. "In order to make documentaries, your brain needs to be 100 percent receptive and open to anything that's going to happen around you. That includes colors and sounds and action and words and especially people," Schwartz explained.

In professions like nursing or engineering, you also have to have imagination, because every single person that you need to help, every person that you need to look after and make well, or every problem you set out to solve, is going to be different. You need to use imagination to take what is already known, what has already been experienced, and what knowledge you have and put it to good use. In science, the most extraordinary breakthroughs are done when scientists have extraordinary imaginations.

"It's a matter of believing," Sarah Stiles told me. "Just saying something and claiming it and believing it — that really can make a lot of things happen. Overcoming the fear thing for sure, just being brave and taking chances, not being afraid to fail, that's a huge thing in acting. As an actor, we're constantly being thrown things to work on. Right now I'm doing a play at night. I've got two readings going on during the day with two huge roles and then I'm working on three concerts that are happening in the next three months. In any given day, I'm wearing ten different hats. But in all of those circumstances, I'm learning a lot and building on this career. And I think that would be applicable to other people too. Just being able to try things."[19]

Part of being confident in using and applying your imagination, particularly when so many others have not yet embraced its possibilities, is to not care what people think. This allows you to pursue the path that seems best to you without worrying about the judgment or criticism. "I think that this is a general principle for any time you want to try something new and different, is that you have to give up a concern with making others happy," suggested Peter McGraw. "The world is set up to get us to behave in a certain way. We learn very early in life that we should care what our parents think about us and what our friends think about us and what the church should think about us and what our government officials would think about us and so on and so forth."

Trying harder or investing more time and energy to find those things that will spark imagination, or lead to a game-changing venture, won't necessarily yield the desired result either. It is easy for people to become so hungry and obsessed with creating something original that they lose perspective, or focus on the wrong things. Taking an idea from imagination to reality certainly requires a level commitment that might border on obsessive, but you also need to step back, consider feedback, and make sure your imagination is fed from the outside as well.

People's imagination flourishes through a multitude of experiences that they have in their life; the more experience the more perspective and the brain matches the things up and weird things come out. Nathan Sawaya, an award-winning artist (famous for creating large-scale sculptures using only LEGO bricks), who started his career as a corporate lawyer, says imagination requires hard work. "You know, so many people sit at the blank computer screen, and wait for inspiration to hit. They wait for their imagination to take hold. Other people just start writing. You either sit and wait for inspiration to strike, or you start doing. And I think doing is what helps imagination take hold. And sometimes, it's just doing a lot of things till one thing really works. And sometimes, it's just starting doing something, and you see a direction and you follow it," he explained.[20]

At the same time, society is structured in a way that drums imagination out. As Peter McGraw explains, "That is true for humor in the sense that we would probably have a lot more comedians and a lot more people who are spending their energy and time doing things in the industry of humor if not for being told as they grew up that that wasn't funny or that wasn't appropriate. Only those who broke through that get to the point where they get to spend their careers working on it and refine their craft."

Nathan Sawaya argues that "We need more exposure to art, just art. Art is not optional," he told me. "I'm not talking about folks spending weeks on a painting or a sculpture like I do. I think there just needs to be a little more creating of art in your daily life .... If people were doing a little more art, you know, finger painting with the kids, or a little doodling here or there, or even snapping Lego bricks together, I think that helps everybody with imagination."

Johanna Schwartz added, "I think people are really scared, scared of losing profits, scared of making their own decisions, scared of impacting negatively upon society as a whole. But if you don't take risks, what's going to happen? I think people are way too concerned with making more and more and more and more money. People are far more concerned with the bottom line than perhaps experimentation and what is experimentation if not imagination made real, made tangible."

"I think that a lot of the ability to have an imagination and utilize it, has to start by not giving a shit," Peter Shankman told me. "When I was growing up I was not a very popular kid — I was the most socially awkward kid you'd ever seen. I didn't have a lot of friends — and would learn very early that my options were to care about what everyone else said and be miserable, or to do what I wanted to do. I think if you look at people who use their imagination it's because they don't care what others think."

Challenge: Collect Stuff. Then Throw It Away

You don't need stuff. You need to interact with it. You need to capture inputs into your brain so you call on them later to form new ideas. So collect lots of things — books and magazines, toys, whatever. Then get rid of it. Call it intentional wastefulness. The key is to add and change your inputs constantly.

To Do: Don't keep things just to keep things. Don't use the same things over and over. Get rid of 10 things in your home and go out and get 10 new things. Then repeat.

Challenge: Analyze a Mistake

If you make a mistake, you should apologize. You should also take a hard look at what went wrong and try to understand what could have gone differently. That's about using your imagination. Remember, it's not the act of making a mistake that invites learning, it is the process of sitting with it, suffering from the consequences — and feeling that pain or discomfort that it causes — that will motivate you to never be in that position again.

To Do: Take any mistake, big or small, and analyze what happened. Don't limit your assessment to just what your experience was — think about how everyone else was impacted, what factors came into play, and how it made other people feel.

NOTES

1. Sutton, R.I. *Weird Ideas that Work*. Free Press, May 15, 2007.
2. Interview with Rita J. King — June 9, 2016.
3. Interview with Peter Shankman — July 29, 2015.
4. http://www.nytimes.com/2008/10/13/arts/television/13war.html
5. http://www.merriam-webster.com/dictionary/centrifugal%20force
6. Interview with Macky Alston — July 29, 2015.
7. Interview with Bradley Feinstein — July 29, 2015.
8. Interview with Sree Sreenivasan — August 17, 2015.
9. Interview with Peter McGaw — October 25, 2015.
10. Interview with Dia Simms — September 14, 2015.
11. Interview with Noah Brier — September 14, 2015.
12. Interview with Johanna Schwartz — October 20, 2015.
13. http://www.campaignlive.co.uk/article/adland-16-part-one-gender/1379217
14. http://www.usatoday.com/story/tech/news/2016/06/30/google-diversity-numbers-2016/86562004/
15. http://www.dalberg.com/wp-content/uploads/2016/06/Diversity_report_6.20.16x.pdf
16. http://www.dailymail.co.uk/sciencetech/article-3252563/Sorry-ladies-Men-seen-creative-women-claims-study.html

17. https://hbr.org/2015/12/even-women-think-men-are-more-creative
18. Interview with Dia Simms — September 14, 2015.
19. Interview with Sarah Stiles — October 20, 2015.
20. Interview with Nathan Sawaya — August 26, 2016.

Smart(er) Data

10

We don't know what to do with all that information we have. There is a lack of understanding about how to interpret and apply that data, what it means, and how to make it valuable. This chapter reconsiders the value of data using imagination as a key driver for how to be smarter about the meaning and opportunity presented by today's connected society. It also outlines specific examples of how data are being used to turn imagination into action in different sectors.

We are awash in data. Organizations collect data from a wide variety of sources, including business transactions, social media, the signals sent by our mobile devices, refrigerators, thermostats, and other devices. Data come in many formats — from structured, numeric data in traditional databases to unstructured text documents, email, video, audio, and maps. The collection of data is still a relatively new phenomenon, so new sources of data are still emerging, and connected devices are introducing new sources of data every day. Even the byproducts of all digital and online activities we complete — log files, cookies, temporary files, and more — often called data exhaust, can be collected, analyzed, and scrutinized to deepen our understanding of what people are doing every day.

But, as Hannah Scott, the Lab Co-coordinator for the Hungry Mind Lab in the United Kingdom, "Imagination is quite an abstract concept; it's generally connected with arts rather than hard science ... so it doesn't actually often cross people's minds to try to pin it down into something concrete. Certainly in science, there have been some attempts to try to better understand it, but no coherent, consistent attempt as of yet."[1] But, we cannot have a complete discussion about imagination and its role in our world without considering data.

Imagination is the ability to see and explore things that don't exist and might not ever be possible, while data provide a detailed record of what has transpired in the course of our lives. The promise of data is precision, while imagination is afforded a certain amount of flexibility in terms of its connection to reality. Imagination and data couldn't be more different. Knowledge, data, facts, figures, theories, and careers are finite. Imagination is infinite. There is no such thing as too much imagination. Is there data that we can use to better understand imagination? What data associated with imagination would be helpful in demonstrating to others what makes new and novel ideas so interesting and valuable?

Data allow us to capture information and mine it for valuable insights that can aid in changing how we think about the world and decide how to act. By considering how data and imagination are related, we can begin to shift the focus of the conversation away from just the existence of data and more toward what data makes possible and what might be worth exploring in the future. So, how does data contribute to our use and application of imagination, and how might data be used to measure imagination and how it is being used?

Quantifying the amount of information that exists in the world is impossible. All we know for sure is that there is an awful lot of data, and more and more is being generated every nanosecond. As we start to get a handle on all that data we are learning new things — pinpointing business trends, identifying and discovering how to prevent diseases, combatting crime, and much more.

Imagination Fueled by Data, and Vice Versa

On September 22, 1999, *The West Wing* premiered on NBC. The television series, which was created and written by Aaron Sorkin, was set primarily in *The West Wing* of the White House during the fictitious Democratic administration of Josiah Bartlet (played by Martin Sheen). *The West Wing* received widespread critical acclaim from critics, political science professors, and former White House staffers. It was also watched, in its inaugural season and the six that followed, by millions of fans around the world — and is said to have inspired a generation of young people to go work on political campaigns, including many who helped to elect President Obama in 2008.

On February 1, 2013, *House of Cards* debuted on Netflix, the streaming video service. The television series, which was created by Beau Willmon, was adapted from a miniseries of the same name set in Britain. It is set in present-day Washington, DC, and follows Frank Underwood (played by Kevin Spacey), a Democrat from South Carolina's 5th congressional district and House Majority Whip, who orchestrates an elaborate plan to become President, aided by his wife, Claire Underwood (played by Robin Wright). The series, which celebrates the dark arts and ruthless quest for power in today's politics, has earned widespread critical acclaim and enjoys a loyal, audience following. The first season was nominated for 13 Primetime Emmy Awards and 4 Golden Globe Awards, the first online only show to ever receive any such nominations.

The West Wing aired on television network so its episodes were introduced on a weekly basis over the course of the television season (September through June). Ratings were measured for each episode, and until the end of each season it was not known for sure whether the series would be renewed for the next year. By contrast, Netflix released the entire season of *House of Cards* episodes on the premiere date and is able to measure the performance of the show in real time. Within days of the premiere, and in some cases even before the new season was available for streaming, Netflix announced plans to produce another season.

When *House of Cards* was first pitched to Netflix, the streaming video company wasn't in the original content business. They had, however, collected a staggering amount of information on their own viewers' usage patterns and had a detailed understanding of their interests. For example, research showed a significant overlap between three different groups of Netflix users:

- Fans of the original BBC miniseries *House of Cards*, produced in 1990;

- Fans of director David Fincher, who was involved with the project from the beginning;

- Fans of Kevin Spacey, who was Fincher's first choice for the lead role.[2]

Netflix was so confident that the new show, once produced, would resonate with the Netflix audience, that they bucked the traditional approach to creating television shows and committed to producing two years of the show without seeing a single minute of footage.

Netflix isn't the only company using data to inform its plans to create the next great television show. Amazon is also in the television business and has been using its data to determine what types of shows would resonate best with their audience early on. Amazon's approach was different — they held a contest for new ideas, and then created pilot episodes for eight different shows drawn from the submissions. The pilots were made available online for free and watched by millions of viewers (or not watched as the case may be). Amazon then used the data to determine what made the different shows successful. After crunching millions of data points, they identified the ingredients they believed would come together to form a hit show.

The result of their analysis was a sitcom about four Republican U.S. senators called *Alpha House*. But the show did not do well as *House of Cards*. Why not?

Sebastian Wernicke, a Germany-based data scientist analyzed the two approaches. In a TEDx Cambridge talk in June of 2015, Wernicke suggested that two steps are needed when using data to create a successful television program: (1) you have to take the data apart and analyze it, and (2) you have to put the data back together and make good use of it. "The crucial thing is that data and data analysis is only good for the first part," he explained in his talk, "It's not suited to put those pieces back together again, and then to come to a conclusion."[3]

Referring to what was needed to get the second step right, Wernicke offered the following:

> There's another tool that can do that, and we all have it. It's the brain," he said. "If there's one thing the brain is good at, it's taking bits and pieces back together again, even when you have to complete information and come to a conclusion. Especially if it's the brain of an expert, and that's why I think Netflix was so successful. They used data and brains where they belong in the process.

House of Cards offers one of the best examples of how big data is being used to understand consumer behavior and shape business decisions with greater intelligence. The success of the show demonstrates that organizations can use data to inform their decisions, not just identify trends and patterns and the opportunities that they present. To be successful, the Netflix team included people who were able to ask the right questions and make sense of the billions of disjointed data points to craft meaningful insights. Most importantly, once the data have been collected and analyzed, the *House of Cards* team was able to use the insights to create something new and compelling that people wanted to consume (and because they are a business, also pay for). Imagination is the ingredient that connected all those key elements, by introducing new opportunities that other shows would not have considered — and that contributed to the success of *House of Cards*.

Data without Imagination

There are many more examples where imagination has not been sufficiently applied to a data project — and the outcomes reflected the lack of a special ingredient.

In 2009, Google announced that they were able to use analysis of data from their Google searches to predict outbreaks of influenza. The essential idea of the project, which was called Google Flu Tracker, was that the results of Google searches showed that people who were looking online for flu-related information provide almost instant evidence of overall flu prevalence. In a paper in the science journal, *Nature* explaining the project, Google argued that search data, if properly integrated with flu tracking information from the Centers for Disease Control and Prevention, for example, could produce accurate estimates of flu prevalence as much as two weeks earlier than the CDC alone. For the first few years, Google Flu Tracker was a major success, and a source of Internet fascination. In 2013, Google Flu Tracker failed, failing to measure or predict the peak of the flu season, missing on their estimates by nearly 140%.

In 2014, a group of scientists from Northeastern University, the University of Houston, and Harvard University compared the performance of Google Flu Tracker with models based on the CDC's data to determine the reasons behind the failure. Their results, which were published in *Nature* and then summarized in an essay in *Wired* magazine, described one of the main failures on the part of Google as "big data hubris." The researchers explained that "… while Google's efforts in projecting the flu were well meaning, they were remarkably opaque in terms of method and data—making it dangerous to rely on Google Flu Trends for any decision-making."[4]

The researchers also suggested that Google undermined its own work by constantly tweaking its search product, including more recommended searches and automated answers to questions, to improve its business and provide more relevant results. They wrote:

> Google's algorithm was quite vulnerable to overfitting to seasonal terms unrelated to the flu, like "high school basketball." With millions of search terms being fit to the CDC's data, there were bound to be searches that were strongly correlated by pure chance, and these

terms were unlikely to be driven by actual flu cases or predictive of future trends. Google also did not take into account changes in search behavior over time. After the introduction of GFT, Google introduced its suggested search feature as well as a number of new health-based add-ons to help people more effectively find the information they need. While this is great for those using Google, it also makes some search terms more prevalent, throwing off GFT's tracking.

In other words, the practice of constantly optimizing their search function to return more precise results to users made it more difficult for the Google Flu Tracker to identify other factors that might be relevant. The algorithms that performed so well for Google in other capacities, such as optimizing search results or serving contextually relevant ads, failed because they were unable to recognize the context surrounding the flu. Google Flu Tracker was developed by humans, so it was only programmed with as much capacity for imagination as the developers introduced when it was launched. Algorithms don't have an imagination of their own, so when the system was left to run on its own, it didn't have the ability to consider new options. The humans involved failed to use or apply their imaginations as well, instead prioritizing efficiency.

Now let's think about the example of *The West Wing* through that same lens. Aaron Sorkin and the team behind *The West Wing* were able to create something that was enjoyed by millions of fans. But NBC didn't have data like today's media companies do. They relied on their imagination to create a fictional political reality that fans ultimately found appealing. Amazon and Google seemingly relied too heavily on their data, failing to employ their imagination that could have surfaced options that algorithms alone were not capable of offering. Meanwhile, Netflix used all the data it collects on its viewers to determine what they might like to see — and that data helped inspire the creators of their new show. Even more importantly for Netflix, that new show (and the many other like it), also generates more, new and different data, which feeds the imagination of more people. The data and the imagination are both critical to the success, on their own and when combined, and continually feed each other.

Imagination and the Fourth Industrial Revolution

Klaus Schwab, the Founder and Executive Chairman of the World Economic Forum (which hosts its annual conference in Davos, Switzerland, attracting policymakers, influential business leaders, and other major players in the global economy), gave the current transformation of our society the name "The Fourth Industrial Revolution." As he explained in the introduction to his book (also titled *The Fourth Industrial Revolution*), "We stand on the brink of a technological revolution that will fundamentally alter the way we live, work, and relate to one another. In its scale, scope, and complexity, the transformation will be unlike anything humankind has experienced before."

For those of you who need a refresher on the previous industrial revolutions: The First Industrial Revolution used water and steam power to mechanize production, the Second used electric power to create mass production, and the Third used electronics and information technology to automate production. The Fourth Industrial Revolution represents a blurring of the lines between physical, digital, and biological elements of our life. We are, essentially, becoming one with the technology (and vice versa).

The exact impact of this transformation, according to Schwab is unclear:

> We have yet to grasp fully the speed and breadth of this new revolution. Consider the unlimited possibilities of having billions of people connected by mobile devices, giving rise to unprecedented processing power, storage capabilities and knowledge access. Or think about the staggering confluence of emerging technology breakthroughs, covering wide-ranging fields such as artificial intelligence (AI), robotics, the Internet of Things (IoT), autonomous vehicles, 3D printing, nanotechnology,

biotechnology, materials science, energy storage and quantum computing, to name a few. Many of these innovations are in their infancy, but they are already reaching an inflection point in their development as they build on and amplify each other in a fusion of technologies across the physical, digital and biological worlds.[5]

There are a lot of people who fear what might happen when machines are given more influence and control over our lives. But there are also strong arguments for the benefits of this more significant melding of our worlds. For example, as technology improves, so does access to health care, resulting in critical advances in biotechnology, not to mention innovations like safer self-driving cars. Similarly, when a society becomes increasingly free of disability or disease, people are better able to learn, and have greater access to education, which leads to increases in political freedom as well. Greater security and political freedom means more stable and peaceful societies, which in turn encourage economic growth and prosperity. It becomes a virtuous cycle of health, education, peace, and prosperity.

As Schwab notes in his book: "In the end, it all comes down to people and values. We need to shape a future that works for all of us by putting people first and empowering them. In its most pessimistic, dehumanized form, the Fourth Industrial Revolution may indeed have the potential to 'robotize' humanity and thus to deprive us of our heart and soul. But as a complement to the best parts of human nature—creativity, empathy, stewardship—it can also lift humanity into a new collective and moral consciousness based on a shared sense of destiny. It is incumbent on us all to make sure the latter prevails."

Measuring Imagination

There is great value in using and applying imagination toward all aspects of our society. There is recognition of the big problems that we face. There is a genuine desire to do things differently.

There is also great interest in finding better ways to do things, and to generate the best possible outcomes: stronger businesses, a more educated citizenry, solutions to the complex problems that challenge our society, and a plan for an even better future. At the same time, there are so many possibilities that are not even being considered. Imagination is the key to unlocking all of that potential to change and improve.

Perhaps we need to be able to show that using your imagination will make you happier or healthier. Perhaps, we need to demonstrate that applying imagination will lead to the creation of new markets or generating of revenue. Perhaps, we need to show that, individually and collectively, we are smarter and more capable when our use of imagination increases and improves.

It is not clear what proof people will need to open up and embrace imagination. Whatever our use and application of imagination ultimately makes possible, we will need hard evidence to back up the claims. The data does not exist yet.

According to Hannah Scott, the co-coordinator of the Hungry Mind Lab, we don't have strong metrics around imagination because, "We (psychologists) say that [imagination is] implicit, or latent, which means that we can't directly measure it in the same way that we can measure, for example, how much somebody sweats in response to fear. This makes it very difficult to create an accurate measurement tool for imagination because you instead have to measure a different but related variable that can actually be directly observed."

Scott explained that researchers have tried to get around this problem by using self-reported measures, such as asking people a series of questions about themselves and their imagination. But people don't always have the best insight into their own actions or beliefs. "Currently, we're not even sure whether imagination is a trait (what a person tends to do) or an ability (how well a person can do it)," Scott told me. "This distinction between trait and ability is important, as it influences how you would go about measuring imagination and therefore how you might capture it: typical performance or maximum performance." She added that, "Another problem is that people don't distinguish very well between creativity, visualization and imagination. In everyday language, the three words are used pretty interchangeably but in fact there are some key distinctions between them. So there have been attempts to assess imagination using measures for creativity or visualization, but they haven't in fact been measuring the right thing."

There are some burgeoning efforts to further research and create standards around imagination — the most notable of which are being led and funded by The Imagination Institute, an independent nonprofit based out of Philadelphia that "dedicated to making progress on the measurement, growth, and improvement of imagination across all sectors of society." The Imagination Institute has announced plans to bring together researchers with notable imaginative and creative individuals in academic, cultural, and organizational domains to "discuss and refine our understanding of the domain specificity of imagination and of future funding." They also hosted a grants competition to "test, validate and develop an intervention for imagination and perspective."

The different research projects funded by the Institute will look at ways to measure, and ultimately improve, the capacity for imaginative and creative thought. The Imagination Institute's director, Scott Barry Kaufman, explained, "We spend so much time on standardized testing and measuring the ability to learn what is, but we don't track how much we're developing people's ability to imagine what could be. That has real implications for social and emotional well-being, as well as for peace and compassion. The ability to transport your mind into the mind of others draws on the same mental machinery that it takes to transport your own mind into the future."

4FIT

Darya Zabelina, a cognitive neuroscientist, leads one of the projects funded by The Imagination Institute. She is "developing an imagination quotient scale, which measure different aspects of specifically imagination. We'll be using that scale, and recruiting people with high and low score on the scale. Trying to directly study imagination, rather than creativity."[6]

The official name of her research project is "The Four Factor Imagination Theory (4FIT): Strategy, Methodology, & Anticipated Results." The description is as follows:

> The first goal of the proposed research is to develop an Imagination Quotient (ImQ) scale, which will include the ability to assess a person's entire imagination capacity, as well as four different aspects of imagination, such as frequency of imaginings, complexity (how detailed they are), emotional valance (positive versus negative), and directedness (goal-directed versus "free-floating"). Upon development of the ImQ scale, we will evaluate the relationships between imagination and its sub-factors and academic achievement, creative achievement, divergent thinking, vocational interests, intelligence, and personality based on self-report measures and performance measures in a large international sample. The final stage of the research program will use neuroimaging techniques (fMRI) to examine neural basis of attention in high and low imaginative people.

Zabelina's project is trying to determine the best ways to measure various aspects of imagination, including frequency of use. "For example, we're asking people how often do you find yourself in these sorts of imaginative states? How frequently do you engage in imagination?" Another one is emotional balance. "We're asking people, when you find yourself in imaginative states, are your imaginings more positive, or are the more negative?" Zabelina and her team are still developing some of the measurement standards that will guide the experimentation, but she noted that there are various questions within that scale. "Presumably, some people, when they imagine things, they're more negative, they worry about something, they synthesize about something that is purely negative, and other people's imagination is quite positive, bright, and funny," she offered.

The key outcome of the research will be a quantifiable scale that can be used for comparison purposes. Zabelina acknowledged that creating a standard measurement for imagination carries the risk of making it something it's not. Still, without some kind of metric or standard, Zabelina argues that people will struggle to take research into imagination seriously. "We're creating the scale with 4 different attributes or factors — frequency, complexity, emotional balance, and directiveness (directiveness in terms of do you engage in imagination, purposefully, or do you mind wander, kind of un-directed imagination) — that we can use to understand the connection between imagination and other aspects of people's personalities," she told me. "We want to look at people who score high or low on any one of those factors, or metrics, and then look more to see what are those people like."

Zabelina acknowledges that you can't quantify imagination. "I don't know if we all start with boundless imagination, or if we lose it. We do lose it, but I don't know if it's all equal for everyone when we're born." She also suggested that a straightforward measure of, say, the quantity of imagination might not be useful. "I think there's an interaction between the capacity for imagination, but also, as we develop, as our central lobes develop, we can use the executive functions to manipulate that information. Kids, yes, they have boundless imagination, but sometimes, it might not necessarily be useful or appropriate in certain situations."

The scale that is not being designed so that overall we can decide someone is more or less imaginative than someone else. There is not going to be a score. Rather, the goal is to establish ways to compare different attributes of imagination. "We want to see whether imagination is linked with certain positive outcomes. For example, if somebody is in a classroom staring out the window, imagining things, and they don't do well on math tests, because they weren't paying attention, perhaps we can show that overall, that is ok. Perhaps we can show that imagination influences happiness, or other quality of life influences."

Hannah Scott suggested that since imagination is so key to cognitive development, this kind of research could be applied to education or training programs to help enable people to learn. Another example may be applications in clinical psychology.

> We know that people with Obsessive Compulsive Disorder [OCD] and psychotic conditions such as schizophrenia aren't in complete control of their imaginations. Somebody with OCD tends to imagine negative future scenarios that will happen if they do or don't something, which causes their characteristic ritualization behaviors. Everyone has these worrying thoughts, but people with OCD imagine them so strongly that they feel compelled to do something about them to ease the worry. Somebody in a psychotic state isn't able to distinguished imagined sensory input from real sensory input, which is what causes the delusions and hallucinations that are completely real to the person experiencing them. So in the long term, if we start to understand imagination better and then start to learn how to harness it, then maybe new types of therapy could be developed to better help people with these mental disorders.

Not surprisingly, any attempt to measure imagination on a scale also introduces some judgment about the quality of that which is being measured. But, as Darya Zabelina notes, "We can't say whether it's better or worse to find yourself in certain negative or positive states. We're differentiating these just as a measure. We're not saying that one is better than the other. Then we can use this measure, and see how people who endorse items for their positive imagination, what other items do they endorse on other types of personality scales." The best the research can offer at this point is a way to connect different personality types to different imagination-related behaviors. Over time we'll be able to explore further whether, or how, one affects the other.

One of the things that inspired Zabelina to pursue this research is that, broadly, imagination has not been valued in the same ways as other neurocognitive functions that can be more directly measured. The benefits of creativity, which has been aggressively studied in recent years, are become more clear and quantifiable. The result of that is not just more investment in academic and other research, but greater efforts to integrate the findings into school, work, and other settings. What Zabelina hopes is that her research will be able to yield data that demonstrates the benefit of imagination — not just in the context of creating something like an idea for a new car — but more generally toward personal well-being.

Hannah Scott and her team at the Hungry Mind Lab are thinking beyond that point. "Right now researchers are the most engaged group because we're still trying to figure out the basics of it. Once we can accurately capture imagination, we can work out exactly what it can be applied to and give this knowledge to the rest of the world to run wild with," she told me. But she also acknowledged that there's still a misconception that imagination is only useful if you want to make art or music or writing. "Not true at all. Leaders must be equally as imaginative in order to come up with new directions to take their business or their people to allow progression. Scientists need to be imaginative enough to come up with new questions to ask, and new ways to answer difficult questions."

Everything is informed by data, both directly and indirectly. We have an unprecedented level of sophistication that we can apply — who we target, how we position issues, the best ways to drive action, and better ways to work with partners. What's missing still, however, is an appreciation for how data connections to what is possible in the future — and what we learn from what we can measure from the past and how we can apply it forward to what hasn't happened yet.

Challenge: Play by Yourself

Everything (well, almost everything) is better with someone else involved. But solo time provides you with a variety of learning opportunities — from exploring your environment at your own pace to becoming self-reliant to learning from your mistakes. As an added bonus: solo experiences help to boost your self-esteem.

To Do: Spend a day entirely on your own. Go on a trip by yourself. Don't write or call anyone. Don't invite someone else to join you for lunch or to see a movie. Make every decision on your own. Think only about yourself. Address every challenge and solve every problem you encounter without any assistance.

Challenge: T-Shirt Statements

What you wear makes a statement about who you are and what you believe. When you put words or images onto a t-shirt, you can send a specific message as well. What would you want to say — if you had to wear it on your chest? What do you want people to know? What if you only have room for few words?

To Do: Design a t-shirt each day, every day, for 30 consecutive days. It doesn't have to be fancy — just imagine a plain shirt with words or pictures on it. What statement do you want?

NOTES

1. Interview with Hannah Scott — July 12, 2016.
2. How Netflix is turning viewers into puppets. *Salon.* http://www.salon.com/2013/02/01/how_netflix_is_turning_viewers_into_puppets/
3. http://www.ted.com/talks/sebastian_wernicke_how_to_use_data_to_make_a_hit_tv_show/transcript?language=en

4. Lazer, D. & Kennedy, R. (2015). What we can learn from the epic Failure of Google Flu Trends. *Wired*, October 1, 2015. http://www.wired.com/2015/10/can-learn-epic-failure-google-flu-trends/
5. http://www3.weforum.org/docs/Media/KSC_4IR.pdf
6. Interview with Darya Zabelina — June 27, 2016.

A Different Kind of F-Word

11

Everyone makes mistakes. Success depends on us failing often and forward, with an eye toward the future. This chapter explains the importance of failing faster and forward, and the important role that imagination plays in supporting a culture of failure.

A lot of what is outlined in this book may turn out to be wrong. Maybe some new information will become available after the book is published. Maybe, after further inspection, the way that I formulated a certain concept when I started writing won't map to any current or future reality. Whatever the reason, I'm okay with being wrong. I'm wrong a lot. I haven't kept track, but my gut tells me, I make mistakes much more than often than I get things right. The way mistakes get processed in my brain send the message that whatever happened could have turned out differently — and it would have been best if it had.

> **NOTE.** *I am okay with all that. Thus far I have not found anything that downing a pint of ice cream, making an impulse-driven purchase, or — more constructively — talking through issues with another person, can't help to address — and then make me feel better so I can get back to my day.*

The more ambitious the effort you are involved in, the more likely you are to experience failure, real or perceived. So it also follows logic that the more you use and apply your imagination, the more likely you are to find yourself at odds with something that is happening today, or with someone's beliefs who are different than yours. That will happen in work, with colleagues and clients, and it will happen in life, with friends and family. The bigger you dream, the harder you will fall. But that doesn't mean you should stop dreaming. That is the worst thing you can do.

Why Isn't Anyone Using the F-Word Anymore?

One of my favorite activities is to eavesdrop on people's conversations. I am always curious to learn what people are talking about, and how they think about their experiences. I listen while riding the subway or walking down the street. I listen while sitting in a restaurant or perusing a store. You can learn a lot by overhearing just a few seconds of what someone says on the phone, or to their friend or as they mutter to themselves without paying any attention to others around them.

Most of what I overhear involves some discussion of logistics — where is someone going, what are they preparing to do later in the day, and so on. There are also plenty of discussions about what is happening in the world — politics, sports, culture, weather. And if I get really lucky, I will hear someone talking about what is happening at work or their interactions with friends and family — the personal stuff that reveals more of their true personality.

Over the past few years the theme that dominated the majority of the conversations I have overheard has been failure. People complain, take issue with how things are going in the world, or call out how something has gone terribly wrong. This theme of embracing failure was also present at the media and tech conferences that I attended. There were panels and hashtags, t-shirts, and business strategy books that championed the benefits of failure. Most people also seemed to have embraced the idea that failure was not only inevitable, but on some level valuable. They were interested in finding ways to learn from mistakes so as to not repeat them. People were proud to fail.

But something changed. I haven't been hearing the word failure mentioned nearly as much — and certainly not in a constructive way. Not by a panelist. Not in conversation between two people over an organic smoothie. Not in the media. Failure still gets discussed, but the tone is different now. We are quick to attack and blame and assign responsibility. Failure is not seen as a badge of honor, but rather a deficiency. And the result is that people are not just afraid to fail, but even to talk about it.

Even in the world of startups and technology companies — the segment of the economy where failure was championed the most; the topic is not as present as it was just a few years ago. Discussions about failure have been replaced with advocacy of collaboration (as if those two things aren't also intertwined), or the great benefits of sharing tools like Slack.

What happened? Maybe it was a downturn in the economy or an uptick in political rancor. More likely the answer is that we got lazy. And as we have discussed throughout the book, when we get lazy, we stop using our imagination. We stop pushing and considering what else might be possible and should be pursued. We get comfortable with the status quo and we stay there. We have to do more than just consider, discuss, and acknowledge the value of failure. To break through and have an opportunity to do new things, we have to really do failure right.

Back when failure was a hot topic, and there was more consideration of the benefits that failure offered, there were a few common elements to the discussion:

- We acknowledged that failing is an inevitable part of the important work required to change something, whether that is solving a complex problem that is facing the planet, or shifting our own behavior to kick a bad habit or start out on a new path;

- Given the option, when trying to learn how to adapt or improve, we agreed that it would be far more useful to look at what happens when things fall apart than dwell on mistakes or cast blame; and

- Making the most of failing gets much easier the more you do it and the more support you have in the process. The more you fail, the better you become at failing — and the sooner you can regroup and try again.

That's a pretty big deal if we think about it. At some point we had consensus that a seemingly difficult, potentially uncomfortable conversation about what happens when things did not go as planned would yield valuable insights. We recognized the benefits of failure. Even more striking, when failure was something that we embraced more, there was a general sense of agreement that we would all benefit by failing more, failing smarter, and doing more to maximize the benefits associated with getting things wrong. In other words, once we agreed that failure had merit, we couldn't get enough of it.

We should fail better than we did when failing was a thing. A few years back, we didn't go deeper in our exploration of failure. Perhaps, the fact that there was consensus ultimately doomed the conversation.

Having consensus on the need to fail more, fail smarter, and fail in different ways doesn't do anything to change how we think, how we act, or the work we are doing. Having agreement on those core points is probably why we aren't still talking about this issue as we should. Because if we agree that failing is constructive, but we don't take the necessary steps to really make the most of it, we convince ourselves that we are on track when we aren't. Agreement in principle is not evidence of action. We assumed that our acknowledgment of the fruits of failure would organically result in a noticeably different way of operating — and probably don't realize that it wasn't happening. We didn't imagine that any other options could or should be explored, and as a result we never found ourselves pushing toward a different way of doing things.

The Value of Bad Ideas

Failure is inevitable. We can fail big. We can fail small. We can fail a lot. We can fail a little. The sooner we can increase our rate of failure, however, the more we can learn and the faster we'll be able to make progress. We need to force ourselves to fail.

At some point, everyone has probably heard the expression, "There's no such thing as a bad idea!" It is easily the most common rule of brainstorming. Alex Osborn, considered by many to be the "father of brainstorming," believed that in order to be successful at brainstorming, participants must "suspend judgment." Osborn understood the perils of what happens when people start criticizing ideas in the midst of a session.

Being open to new ideas — tapping into the fully potential of our imagination — also means giving every idea, even ideas that resonate as undeniably "bad" a chance to be considered, debated, and developed. Osborn suggested that we suspend judgment, not eliminate it. We can eventually evaluate and judge whether some ideas are worth considering further, or dismiss them as unacceptable, impractical, or simply off-target. But we must suspend that judgment until an idea has had a chance to percolate or we risk shutting off access to our imagination entirely.

Forcing ourselves, the organizations we work for, the people we work with, the communities we are part of to fail more, to fail smarter, is going to make that whole experience easier. It is going to introduce the tension that we need to unlock our imagination more fully.

With plenty of practice, I have come to feel pretty confident in my ability to learn and adapt when I fail. There is a lot of room for improvement — I fail in new ways and learn new things from those experiences all the time. I do my best to share those lessons as well, so that everyone else can make different mistakes. Of course, I am just one person. The benefits of my failing are limited to my own experiences and individual reach. I can do more to help others understand my mistakes, and what I learned from them. We all can. And when we do, it allows everyone else to focus their energy failing on different things — to make new mistakes and to get smarter.

I challenge you. I implore you. I beg of you. Start failing. Fail on your own. Fail with others. Fail in ways that we all will learn and benefit from.

Challenge: Be Afraid, Be Very Afraid

The trouble with worry, when it does not lead to a solution, is that we end up dealing emotionally with all kinds of bad situations that aren't even occurring. Our imagination can take control of our life. But being scared isn't always a negative. After you survive a scary interaction, the next one isn't so bad. You feel emboldened to take bigger chances and receive bigger payoffs. So why not force yourself to be afraid — so you can figure out how to deal with it?

To Do: Think about something terrible happening. Now think about your response — if you had time to assess the situation and control the outcome. What will you do differently now that you have thought through that scenario? What steps might you take to be prepared in the future for something bad to happen?

Challenge: Analyze a Mistake

If you make a mistake, you should apologize. You should also take a hard look at what went wrong and try to understand what could have gone differently. That's about using your imagination. Remember, it's not the act of making a mistake that invites learning, it is the process of sitting with it, suffering from the consequences — and feeling that pain or discomfort that it causes — that will motivate you to never be in that position again.

To Do: Take any mistake, big or small, and analyze what happened. Don't limit your assessment to just what your experience was — think about how everyone else was impacted, what factors came into play, and how it made other people feel.

Big Ideas and
Big Questions

This chapter outlines a series of specific issues, challenges, and ideas that will only be possible when we learn to use and apply our imagination, and offers a series of questions to help us all think about how to use and apply our imagination differently. Together, these ideas and questions will help us to understand how to move forward and close the imagination gap.

Throughout the book, you have been introduced to various arguments for using and applying your imagination along with some guidance on how to go about beginning the important work of closing the Imagination Gap. At the bottom of each chapter, I have included specific challenges to help encourage you to generate new, imaginative ideas. None of the arguments on their own will likely provide enough evidence for you to completely change your way of thinking or acting.

Part of what this book is about is simply recognizing that imagination is available to us all, and is also on display in so many different ways that we aren't recognizing or celebrating. Could we do a lot more with our imaginations? Absolutely. Would we all benefit from just having greater access to people who are thinking in ways that we never considered? Without a doubt.

This chapter is designed as a bridge — a way to connect how we currently use our imagination (or don't use it enough as the case may be) and the future where our imagination is applied regularly and continuously, wherever you have the opportunities.

After, After the Impact ...

In my last book, *Shift & Reset*, I challenged people to think bigger and change the way we approach how we tackle the most important and complex issues facing our society. I began with a metaphor of a meteorite hurtling toward earth, representing all the challenges that exist for each of us, the organizations we work for, and our society at large if we fail to address the planet's most pressing concerns. In the postscript to the book I explored what would happen if we failed to act, letting the metaphorical meteorite hit us.

Since the book was published in 2010, new discoveries have been made, new perspectives formed and new people have stepped up to try and lead. The desire to change and improve still exists. There are resources available to apply towards solving problems and creating a better future. Innovation remains a buzzword used by leaders across every sector. And yet, really bad things continue to happen. None of the problems that we faced then have been solved and a whole new set of challenges have emerged. The path forward is not entirely clear and the imagination gap prevents us from making the progress that is needed.

Here is the challenge that we must all accept.

We all must learn to embrace how, as individuals and as organizations, the changes that are happening in the world impact our work, our perspectives, and our behaviors. We must learn — and move quickly — to adapt to these changing times. And the timing couldn't be better. The public is more engaged than ever before, more capable of collecting and sharing information with a wider audience — for free — than at any point in our history. This drives greater interest in media and public affairs, politics and business, culture, and art. The creation of a more diverse and interesting culture is in progress.

This isn't simply about having more people sharing stories, displaying their personalities, or building a following because the barriers to entry are lower. This isn't just about finding hidden talent far down the long tail of media and elevating them to the status of super celebrity because the institutional structures that once controlled everything are breaking down. The impact that technology and the Internet are having on all aspects of our society is profound. This is the beginning of a shift that will redefine every aspect of our culture and our society.

We don't get to decide whether we want a new society. The changes underway can't be rolled back, nor contained. The systems and structures that have governed our society, organized our focus, and consumed our energy in the past are no longer functioning well. However, we do get to decide what kind of society we want to live in, what types of solutions we want to pursue, and how we want to function as individuals. And that's a lot of power and opportunity to explore.

There is an abundance of ideas and suggestions for how to address serious issues. There are new formulas and models, platforms, and groups emerging to take on the challenges that exist in our society. But our tendency is to focus on the elements we can control. Too often, individuals return to what they know. Organizations repeat what they have done before. With the serious issues that threaten every facet of our present existence, we do not have the luxury to look back or repeat what we have done before. If what we are doing isn't working anymore, we have to do something different. Everything could be working better, and it is our responsibility to make sure that we get to a place where it does.

We must resist the desire to define or contain this new, emerging culture too quickly, to focus our attention on finding ways to market and monetize it above all. We should think bigger. What is the potential for technology and the Internet to redefine our culture, and what say do we want to have in that? What must be changed, or adapted, within our society to ensure that the solutions that are developed today, the ideas that emerge from the massive and frenetic coordination of people online, or through connections that only recently became available, aren't lost as we head into the future?

The influence of little "m" media (the concept of which I introduced in my first book, *Media Rules!*) — information, experiences, and stuff that we value and desire — remains a powerful force. Gone are the days when the majority of the population will sit for hours to read a newspaper from cover to cover. Our information experiences have changed and our focus and goals in terms of how we address serious issues should change as well. Millions of people will tune in to watch a football game, but the more important collective experiences that could help improve race relations or help support a community in need can't attract the same level of collective interest or participation. What can we do with small, dedicated, passionate audiences? How can we connect communities and individuals, and what would it take to bring together disparate ideas?

In the modern industrial age, efficiency and speed have overtaken quality. But if we think bigger, we can elevate the work that is needed to address serious issues to a place where it influences how we think, act, and perceive everything. We can't only focus on improving what we know or fixing what is broken; we should consider all the possible ways to address an issue, creating the ideas and products, and programs and approaches necessary to do things that have no blueprint to follow or pattern to copy.

The discussion about addressing serious issues and solving complex problems should be bigger — more voices, more access to information, more collaboration. So should our excitement and commitment to creating amazing, transformative, and completely new products, plans, and things to pursue. Fueled by technology, we all have the ability to learn or discuss whatever we believe is relevant, to produce and distribute information so that it reaches audiences any time, any place. Algorithms shape our media consumption habits so that our Facebook feeds are filled with information about topics that relate to our lives, or are suggested by our friends. We can sign up for online courses to supplement our traditional education and complement our professional skills — all on demand, through any device of our choosing. And when there are issues or stories that the mainstream media companies aren't covering to our satisfaction, we can use our smartphone to capture, produce, and stream media and make our voices heard.

We should want a more diverse (and deeply invested) audience, able to connect across any device, so that we don't have to rely exclusively on someone else's channel or community to learn about an issue or take action that has an impact. Instead of a few companies, distributors, creators, or similar, there should be millions. Instead of a relatively small number of people making decisions that impact the masses, we should seek full participation and further democratization of power. We should be looking to support and enhance, cultivate and create a broader commitment to change and a larger vision of what is possible.

Everyone serves as a gatekeeper now, and each of us can be a storyteller. Every person with a blog or cell-phone-enabled camera can deliver information and incite change. Every person with a computer and an Internet connection can demonstrate their imagination to the world. It is happening every day. But a lot of bad content overwhelms and distracts. We spend too much time trying to contain ideas, to define them and channel them to ways of operating we already understand. Instead of unleashing our imagination, we train our focus on innovation and optimization of the things we already know. We try to prioritize stories and concepts because they fit into an established system or can be more easily monetized. We do what we have always done because that is what makes us most comfortable.

What Qualifies as a Big Idea?

Every day there are dozens of announcements claiming a major breakthrough, disruptive innovation or other hyperbolic achievement in technology, health, politics and diplomacy, education, and others facets of our society. Rarely do these grand statements live up to the hype.

Alison Arieff, a contributing opinion writer for *the New York Times*, argues that the reason is because we are oriented to think about these big challenges in the wrong way. She wrote:

> Every day, innovative companies promise to make the world a better place. Are they succeeding? Here is just a sampling of the products, apps and services that have come across my radar in the last few weeks:
>
> - A service that sends someone to fill your car with gas.
>
> - A service that sends a valet on a scooter to you, wherever you are, to park your car.
>
> - A service that will film anything you desire with a drone.
>
> - A service that will pack your suitcase — virtually.
>
> - A service that delivers a new toothbrush head to your mailbox every three months.
>
> - A service that delivers your beer right to your door.
>
> - An app that analyzes the quality of your French kissing.
>
> - A "smart" button and zipper that alerts you if your fly is down.
>
> - An app with speaker that plays music from within a mother's vaginal walls to her unborn baby.
>
> - A sensor placed in your child's diaper that sends you an alert when the diaper needs changing.
>
> - An app that lets us brew our coffee from anywhere.
>
> - A refrigerator advertised as "the Family Hub" that promises to act as a personal assistant, message board, stereo and photo album.

- An app to locate rentable driveways for parking.

- An app to locate rentable yachts.

- An app to help you understand "cause and effect in your life."

- An app that guides mindful meditation.

- An app that imparts wisdom.

- And a new proposal to create an app designed to stop police killings.

In her column,[1] Arieff admonishes entrepreneurs, and especially people in the tech community (Silicon Valley and places like it) for not only ignoring the larger issues that exist, but also convincing themselves that their "innovations" were contributing to some greater good. She also made reference to the "Unexotic Underclass" a term used by Nnaemeka to describe single mothers, veterans returning from combat in Iraq and Afghanistan, 50 + year old workers whose needs are either being overlooked, or underserved, by the so-called great innovators of our time.

In an essay for MIT Entrepreneurship Review,[2] Nnaemeka wrote:

> The space that caters to my demographic — the cushy 20 and 30-something urbanites — is oversaturated. It's not rocket science: people build what they know. Cosmopolitan, well-educated young men and women in America's big cities are rushing into startups and building for other cosmopolitan well-educated young men and women in big cities. If you need to plan a trip, book a last minute hotel room, get your nails done, find a date, get laid, get an expert shave, hail a cab, buy clothing, borrow clothing, customize clothing, and share the photos instantly, you have Hipmunk, HotelTonight, Manicube, OKCupid, Grindr, Harry's, Uber, StyleSeek, Rent the Runway, eshakti/Proper Cloth and Instagram respectively to help you. These companies are good,

with solid brains behind them, good teams and good funding.

But there are only so many suit customization, makeup sampling, music streaming, social eating, discount shopping, experience curating companies that the market can bear. *If you're itching to start something new, why chase the nth iteration of a company already serving the young, privileged, liberal jetsetter? If you're an investor, why revisit the same space as everyone else?* There is life, believe me, outside of NY, Cambridge, Chicago, Atlanta, Austin, L.A. and San Fran.

It's where the unexotic underclass lives. It's called America.

Nnaemeka published her article on May 19, 2013. Alison Arieff published her op-ed on July 10, 2016. What has changed in the three-plus years between the articles being published? It appears not very much.

The challenges facing our society are growing more severe. No matter the issue — climate change, education, poverty, hunger, etc. — no matter how much money and time are invested, little progress is being made. No matter the sector — business, media, nonprofits, and so on — we are still largely operating as they have for generations, and are unprepared for the speed of change in our society. The urgency felt across all sectors and around all issues is real. But our response is inadequate. We spend too much time telling stories, celebrating activity, and raising awareness about the need to take action, instead of thinking more broadly, being more nimble, focusing on the future, and actually changing how things are done. Things will continue to get worse unless we quickly change our approach — and there are real consequences if that happens.

Doug Rauch, who spent 31 years with Trader Joe's Company, the last 14 years as President, helping grow the business from a small, nine-store chain in Southern California, to a nationally acclaimed retail success story, says one of the most critical things to decide is how to apply imagination. "The question is: Do we funnel imagination? Do we channel it? Do we utilize it?" he told me.[3] "It's not imagination in itself — in my opinion it's not enough. It's how do you use it? How do you take that energy and turn it into something that is actually of value from a product business service standpoint," he continued. Rauch used his own experience with Trader Joe's to explain further.

What Trader Joe's looked at in response to a market challenge which is how does a small company survive against these great, big behemoths. It had to reinvent a number of things. Reinvent how private labels are really done, reinvent how a product is purchased, reinvent what private label means to a customer. Instead of it just being a lower quality product at a cheaper price, Trader Joe's actually went out and created destination products and offered a store brand that people look at as a viable competitor to a national brand. That had not really been done in any way at scale or certainly in the manner that Trader Joe's went about doing it. So in an area like that I would say that most people would've looked at that field and gone that's not a field for imagination or innovation, but it has certainly worked out.

Rauch explained that oftentimes imagination is not enough by itself because you have to know something about the limits of either the instrument or the techniques you're using, along with your imagination. That is true for business, as well as in the arts or other creative categories, or when taking on significant social challenges.

Curing cancer is an example of a big idea. Improving treatment or reducing the number of cases of people battling cancer doesn't qualify as a big idea. That is still tremendously important and a worthwhile challenge that needs to be met, a series of innovations that should be pursued. But the big idea is that we can, and will, completely end cancer: all 200+ different variations of cancer — gone. The goal needs to be that big, that imaginative.

But, as Dia Simms offered, "We don't have cures anymore. There is no one coming up with any types of cures. We are approaching medicine in a very much unimaginative way."[4]

Other big ideas might include producing and equally distributing food across the globe so that nobody goes hungry. Ever. Getting 100% of eligible voters in the United States to turn out and cast a ballot on Election Day. Giving every person, regardless of race, religion, gender, or any other classification, the same equal rights, equal protections, and equal opportunities to thrive. Making it possible for the 60+ million people around the world (and growing) who have been forced to flee their homes because of violence or persecution, and as a result qualify as refugees, can return home safely, or be welcomed into other countries. Doing whatever it takes so there no more innocent people are killed by gun violence or terrorism.

Big ideas don't only have to be about stopping bad things from happening. Flying cars would be an amazing achievement. If my Seattle Mariners were to win the World Series, we would achieve something that nobody alive today has seen before. Anything we can dream up, or decide to create, can go on this list. There is no judge or special counsel who decides whether an idea qualifies as new or exciting enough — but we should all want to strive for things that go beyond what we can currently comprehend. We should use and apply our imagination to conceive of a future that is better than what we know in the present.

These may seem like impossible challenges. But that's where the best ideas start. Most people won't even entertain a serious conversation about goals that large. That's partly what qualifies them as big ideas — and worthy of consideration. Of course there are practical issues. There are a limited number of hours in the day, and a limited number of dollars. We don't even know what expertise we will need to draw on, or if that expertise is even currently available, to pursue an idea that we haven't yet considered. But none of those practical issues should limit your imagination, so there is no reason such big ideas shouldn't be explored and considered.

In an era of too many demands and too much information, it can seem foolish, or wasteful, to think of more and bigger ideas. But that's exactly what our imagination is for, and why it's so important we use and apply our imagination at every possible opportunity. We don't know what the future will require, or offer, and we should think about everything we might possibly want to consider exploring. Thinking about big ideas is one of the best ways to determine what we really believe to be important, and what we want to prioritize as we move ahead. The minute we stop thinking big is the minute we settle for less than we are capable of achieving.

Questions, Questions, Questions

I have attended a good number of hackathons, pitch competitions, and other similar events where entrepreneurs (or similar) are challenged to develop and present their new ideas for solving a problem, of any kind (business, humanitarian, purely hypothetical). On a few occasions I have been the one on stage trying to show that my idea is the best. Mostly, however, I am invited to be one of the people who decides which concept has the most promise and which team (or individual) would benefit most from money or other support. By design, the presentations are kept short and the amount of information shared is limited. We are expected to make a snap decision and identify the right choice to name the winner.

I don't know how to make a good snap judgment. I can certainly form opinions and am not shy about voicing them, but the ones that come together in the shortest amount of time and with the least input considered are almost always the most foolish. Go figure. So instead, I take a different approach and try instead to ask questions. I ask questions of the presenters. I share questions with my fellow judges. I might post a question online to prompt a response from someone who isn't even in the room to hear the pitch.

Without fail, I always have more questions than I am given time to ask. So I thought I would share some of the questions I have collected over the years, to see what kind of new thinking they might spark. Here you go:

> Q: How do you pull multiple streams of data (make multiple calls) — from various sources — more effectively? Do you build an internal data storage capacity? Is there benefit if you create a centralized data repository of some kind that many can easily access?

> Q: How do you turn non-changemakers into changemakers? Can you teach someone a new approach, or do you have to build your teachers from scratch?

> Q: What helps people overcome the barrier to entry/starting? Framing? Education? What do they need to think about to get people to embrace this data stream?

> Q: There are always super-users for anything — but how do you get 'normal people' to provide insights that could help to craft the tool and position it for success?

> Q: Is there a way to commercialize a product WITHOUT selling it (and instead get the value of the data that is collected)?

> Q: What are the new, most interesting ways that different brands/organizations are getting people to support a discussion about a serious issue?

> Q: What are the connections between climate change and other aspects of life that can be used to provide context, access to new/different audiences?

> Q: Can you take the idea of 'partnership' or 'collaboration' to the next level? Is there an opportunity (or benefit) to creating a truly shared brand — a 'super friends' unit for trying to accomplish something?

Q: What is the BIG, FUTURE of news — the things that nobody is thinking about?

Q: How can data help tell us what people will be curious about next — instead of just making us better at responding? How can we predict trends that aren't based on past behaviors?

Q: How do you get people who don't understand something like Virtual Reality to embrace it (and make the whole conversation a bit more mainstream to reach more people)? How do you create more 'consumer' demand (which will then drive media adoption, etc) for something complicated and somewhat obscure?

Asking questions generates more engagement than offering feedback. Questions challenge people to think differently, to consider new options. They spark our imagination and lead us into unfamiliar territory.

Of course, a spark in the imagination doesn't come with every question. For that we need to ask challenging questions. We have to keep pushing. As Isaac Luria, a movement leader and faith organization, told me:

> You have to go down the road with someone over and over again. And it sometimes makes people very pissed. But you push through that, you keep asking the questions because you are trying to deeper and deeper.
>
> "What are you after? If you can have everything in the world, snap your finger and what would you have?" And usually what happens towards the end of the exercise, after you get through the frustration moment, and the laughing, and the sort of discomfort of everybody watching this in the room, and it usually takes between 10 and 15 minutes, is that somebody starts to articulate a vision of what they would like the world to look like.

They start to paint a picture of the street that they live on, the picnic table out back in their yard. They start to paint a picture of the people that are there and what their facial expressions are.

Luria says he likes to start people off with questions that make people think about human level details. "I usually begin by asking people to imagine the world where they have achieved whatever their goal is ... 'What do people's faces look like? Is there food there? Who is there? What do they look like?' And the vision that comes across is one that is way more universal than anything that they're thinking about as an organizer."

Luria adds that the questions help to shift people's thinking, as well as how they communicate. He also joked "the whole room is usually crying by the end of it — but that's because the vision is so much clearer." By answering those questions, they figure out what they are fighting for.

Would You like to Play a Game?

Questions is a game that is played by participants maintaining a dialogue of asking questions back and forth for as long as possible, without making any declarative statements. You can play by yourself, but it's better with an opponent. Questions can be played in a group, but with more people involved, each player has more time to think, and the pressure is not as great.

It's a bit like tennis. Play begins when the first player serves by asking a question. The second player must respond to the question with another question. Each player must quickly continue the conversation by using only questions. You can't hesitate, make a declarative statement, or ask a question that is unrelated to the topic being volleyed — if (or when) a player responds with anything but another question, they have committed a foul and their opponent wins the point.

Questions is a classic improv exercise. It can also be an effective way for anyone, in any sector, to build a story and expand on an idea. It is a tool employed by comedians when engaging with a heckler. Lawyers and police officers are specially trained to ask questions (though I don't suppose they think of it as a game in most cases). Politicians usually struggle to play — they prefer to provide answers (statements that don't actually answer the question) instead of returning serve. I'm surprised there isn't an app-based competition version — like Words with Friends, but for asking questions.

Asking questions — whether you play the game or not — is one of the best ways to prompt you to use and apply your imagination. The game challenges you to break out your normal way of thinking. Our natural instinct is to want to resolve a disagreement, to win an argument, or convince another person that our view is best. But, *Questions* isn't about ending the conversation — you win by lobbying new inquiries back to the other person. You succeed by keeping the conversation going and pushing your thinking further and further. You can't control the tone or focus — your only choice is to accept the idea that has been offered and generate a question in response. There are no right answers. In fact there are no answers at all, just more questions.

Would you like to play a game of questions with me? Email me your response ... brian@theimaginationgap.com

---

Challenge: Play a Game

Chutes and Ladders, Monopoly, Cards against Humanity, and Bingo: there are thousands of games — including plenty that is probably attracting dust in a closet somewhere in your home — that will feed your imagination and spark new kinds of thinking. You can play alone, or with friends and family. You can play them one at a time, or put together a modern pentathlon of gaming. All you need to do is start playing.

To Do: Pick a game. Play it. Then do it again (with the same game, or another, it doesn't matter).

Challenge: Take a Noticing Tour

Most of the time when we go for a walk (or a drive, train ride, airplane flight, or similar), our goal is to get from one place to another. We travel with a purpose and don't take the time to look at the surroundings as we pass. When we do look around, we notice things. And just noticing various things as you walk down the street can be more powerful than it might seem. The noticing — paying attention to what you see, hear, feel, taste, and smell — brings you into the present time. It feeds your imagination with new ideas and inputs.

To Do: Go for a walk. You don't need to have a destination in mind or impose time or distance requirements. Just walk, and look around, and notice things.

NOTES

1. http://www.nytimes.com/2016/07/10/opinion/sunday/solving-all-the-wrong-problems.html)
2. http://miter.mit.edu/the-unexotic-underclass
3. Interview with Doug Rauch — August 27, 2016.
4. Interview with Dia Simms — September 14, 2015.

Index